DOVER·THRIFT·EDITIONS

Complete Poems

CHRISTOPHER MARLOWE

DOVER PUBLICATIONS, INC.
Mineola, New York

DOVER THRIFT EDITIONS

GENERAL EDITOR: PAUL NEGRI

EDITOR OF THIS VOLUME: DREW SILVER

Copyright

Bibliographical Note

This Dover edition, first published in 2003, contains all Marlowe's English-language poems, unabridged, taken from a standard edition. *Ovid's Elegies* and "The Passionate Shepherd to His Love" date from 1581–1584; *Hero and Leander* and *Lucan's First Book* from 1592–1593. The Publisher's Note was prepared especially for this edition.

Library of Congress Cataloging-in-Publication Data

Marlowe, Christopher, 1564–1593.
  [Poems]
  Complete poems / Christopher Marlowe.
     p. cm. — (Dover thrift editions)
  Contents: Ovid's elegies — The passionate shepherd to his love — Hero and Leander — Lucan's first book.
  ISBN 0-486-42674-2
  I. Title.

PR2662 2003
821'.3—dc21

2002034822

Manufactured in the United States of America
Dover Publications, Inc., 31 East 2nd Street, Mineola, N.Y. 11501

Note

This volume contains all of Marlowe's extant poetry in English. The translations from Ovid and "The Passionate Shepherd to His Love" are believed to date from Marlowe's years at Cambridge in the early 1580s; the translation from Lucan's *Civil War* and *Hero and Leander*, based on the work of the fifth-century Greek poet Musaeus (widely circulated in Latin translation in the sixteenth century) from a later date. Marlowe is believed to have written more lyrics such as "The Passionate Shepherd," but none survives. *Hero and Leander* was left unfinished at Marlowe's reported death in 1593. It was continued by George Chapman, who published the completed work; only the section Marlowe finished is included here.

Christopher Marlowe (1564–1593) was born at Canterbury, son of a shoemaker. He attended school and university on scholarships. After taking his master's degree at Cambridge, Marlowe declined to take holy orders and became involved in the literary and theatrical worlds of Elizabethan London. Known primarily as a playwright, Marlowe was a brilliant and powerful dramatic writer, the greatest master of blank verse before Shakespeare. Among his most notable works for the stage are *Tamburlaine the Great*, Parts I and II, *The Jew of Malta*, and *The Tragical History of Doctor Faustus*. From the time Marlowe was a student, he is believed to have worked for the secret intelligence service operated for the Elizabethan government by Sir Francis Walsingham; this involvement is believed to have contributed to the disputed circumstances of his reported violent death in 1593. Most scholars accept that Marlowe was killed at this time, but there is disagreement as to why; some believe that his death may have been staged. All theories regarding his fate are unfortunately impossible to prove with the known evidence.

Contents

Ovid's Elegies: Book One

ELEGIA I
Quemadmodum a Cupidine pro bellis amoris scribere coactus sit

We which were Ovid's five books now are three,
For these before the rest preferreth he;
If reading five thou plain'st of tediousness,
Two ta'en away, thy labour will be less.
With Muse prepared I meant to sing of arms,
Choosing a subject fit for fierce alarms.
Both verses were alike till Love (men say)
Began to smile and took one foot away.
Rash boy, who gave thee power to change a line?
We are the Muses' prophets, none of thine.
What if thy mother take Diana's bow?
Shall Dian fan when Love begins to glow?
In woody groves is 't meet that Ceres reign,
And quiver-bearing Dian till the plain?
Who'll set the fair-tressed Sun in battle ray,
While Mars doth take the Aonian harp to play?
Great are thy kingdoms, over-strong and large,
Ambitious imp, why seek'st thou further charge?
Are all things thine? The Muses' Tempe thine?
Then scarce can Phoebus say, 'This harp is mine.'
When in this work's first verse I trod aloft,
Love slacked my muse, and made my numbers soft.
I have no mistress nor no favourite,
Being fittest matter for a wanton wit.
Thus I complained, but Love unlocked his quiver,

Took out the shaft, ordained my heart to shiver,
And bent his sinewy bow upon his knee,
Saying, 'Poet, here's a work beseeming thee.'
O woe is me! He never shoots but hits;
I burn, Love in my idle bosom sits.
Let my first verse be six, my last five feet;
Farewell stern war, for blunter poets meet.
Elegian muse, that warblest amorous lays,
Girt my shine brow with sea-bank myrtle sprays.

ELEGIA II
Quod primo amore correptus, in triumphum duci se a Cupidine patiatur

What makes my bed seem hard seeing it is soft?
Or why slips down the coverlet so oft?
Although the nights be long, I sleep not tho,
My sides are sore with tumbling to and fro.
Were Love the cause, it's like I should descry him,
Or lies he close, and shoots where none can spy him?
'Twas so, he struck me with a slender dart,
'Tis cruel Love turmoils my captive heart.
Yielding or struggling do we give him might;
Let's yield, a burden easily borne is light.
I saw a brandished fire increase in strength,
Which being not shaked, I saw it die at length.
Young oxen newly yoked are beaten more
Than oxen which have drawn the plough before;
And rough jades' mouths with stubborn bits are torn,
But managed horses' heads are lightly borne.
Unwilling lovers love doth more torment
Than such as in their bondage feel content.
Lo, I confess, I am thy captive I,
And hold my conquered hands for thee to tie.
What need'st thou war? I sue to thee for grace;
With arms to conquer armless men is base.
Yoke Venus' doves, put myrtle on thy hair,
Vulcan will give thee chariots rich and fair;
The people thee applauding, thou shalt stand,
Guiding the harmless pigeons with thy hand;
Young men and women shalt thou lead as thrall,
So will thy triumph seem magnifical.

I, lately caught, will have a new-made wound,
And captive-like be manacled and bound;
Good Meaning, Shame, and such as seek love's wrack
Shall follow thee, their hands tied at their back.
Thee all shall fear, and worship as a king,
Io triumphing shall thy people sing.
Smooth Speeches, Fear and Rage shall by thee ride,
Which troops have always been on Cupid's side;
Thou with these soldiers conquerest gods and men,
Take these away, where is thine honour then?
Thy mother shall from heaven applaud this show,
And on their faces heaps of roses strow.
With beauty of thy wings, thy fair hair gilded,
Ride, golden Love, in chariots richly builded.
Unless I err, full many shalt thou burn,
And give wounds infinite at every turn.
In spite of thee, forth will thine arrows fly,
A scorching flame burns all the standers by.
So, having conquered Ind, was Bacchus' hue;
Thee pompous birds, and him two tigers drew.
Then seeing I grace thy show in following thee,
Forbear to hurt thyself in spoiling me.
Behold thy kinsman's Caesar's conquering bands,
Who guards the conquered with his conquering hands.

ELEGIA III
Ad amicam

I ask but right: let her that caught me late
Either love, or cause that I may never hate.
I ask too much: would she but let me love her;
Love knows with such like prayers I daily move her.
Accept him that will serve thee all his youth,
Accept him that will love with spotless truth.
If lofty titles cannot make me thine,
That am descended but of knightly line
(Soon may you plough the little land I have;
I gladly grant my parents given to save),
Apollo, Bacchus and the Muses may,
And Cupid, who hath marked me for thy prey,
My spotless life, which but to gods gives place,
Naked simplicity, and modest grace.

I love but one, and her I love change never,
If men have faith, I'll live with thee for ever.
The years that fatal destiny shall give
I'll live with thee, and die, ere thou shalt grieve.
Be thou the happy subject of my books,
That I may write things worthy thy fair looks.
By verses hornèd Io got her name,
And she to whom in shape of swan Jove came,
And she that on a feigned bull swam to land,
Griping his false horns with her virgin hand.
So likewise we will through the world be rung,
And with my name shall thine be always sung.

ELEGIA IV
*Amicam, qua arte, quibusve nutibus in caena, praesente viro uti
debeat, admonet*

Thy husband to a banquet goes with me,
Pray God it may his latest supper be.
Shall I sit gazing as a bashful guest,
While others touch the damsel I love best?
Wilt lying under him, his bosom clip?
About thy neck shall he at pleasure skip?
Marvel not, though the fair bride did incite
The drunken Centaurs to a sudden fight;
I am no half-horse, nor in woods I dwell,
Yet scarce my hands from thee contain I well.
But how thou shouldst behave thyself now know,
Nor let the winds away my warnings blow.
Before thy husband come, though I not see
What may be done, yet there before him be.
Lie with him gently, when his limbs he spread
Upon the bed, but on my foot first tread.
View me, my becks and speaking countenance;
Take and receive each secret amorous glance.
Words without voice shall on my eyebrows sit,
Lines thou shalt read in wine by my hand writ.
When our lascivious toys come in thy mind,
Thy rosy cheeks be to thy thumb inclined.
If aught of me thou speak'st in inward thought,
Let thy soft finger to thy ear be brought.
When I (my light) do or say aught that please thee,

Turn round thy gold ring, as it were to ease thee.
Strike on the board like them that pray for evil,
When thou dost wish thy husband at the devil.
What wine he fills thee, wisely will him drink;
Ask thou the boy what thou enough dost think.
When thou hast tasted, I will take the cup,
And where thou drink'st, on that part I will sup.
If he gives thee what first himself did taste,
Even in his face his offered gobbets cast.
Let not thy neck by his vile arms be pressed,
Nor lean thy soft head on his boist'rous breast.
Thy bosom's roseate buds let him not finger,
Chiefly on thy lips let not his lips linger.
If thou givest kisses, I shall all disclose,
Say they are mine and hands on thee impose.
Yet this I'll see, but if thy gown aught cover,
Suspicious fear in all my veins will hover.
Mingle not thighs nor to his leg join thine,
Nor thy soft foot with his hard foot combine.
I have been wanton, therefore am perplexed,
And with mistrust of the like measure vexed.
I and my wench oft under clothes did lurk,
When pleasure moved us to our sweetest work.
Do not thou so, but throw thy mantle hence,
Lest I should think thee guilty of offence.
Entreat thy husband drink, but do not kiss,
And while he drinks, to add more do not miss;
If he lies down with wine and sleep oppressed,
The thing and place shall counsel us the rest.
When to go homewards we rise all along,
Have care to walk in middle of the throng;
There will I find thee or be found by thee,
There touch whatever thou canst touch of me.
Aye me, I warn what profits some few hours,
But we must part when heav'n with black night lours.
At night thy husband clips thee: I will weep
And to the doors sight of thyself keep.
Then will he kiss thee, and not only kiss,
But force thee give him my stol'n honey bliss.
Constrained against thy will, give it the peasant;
Forbear sweet words, and be your sport unpleasant.
To him I pray it no delight may bring,

Or if it do, to thee no joy thence spring;
But though this night thy fortune be to try it,
To me tomorrow constantly deny it.

ELEGIA V
Corinnae concubitus

In summer's heat, and mid-time of the day,
To rest my limbs upon a bed I lay;
One window shut, the other open stood,
Which gave such light as twinkles in a wood,
Like twilight glimpse at setting of the sun,
Or night being past, and yet not day begun.
Such light to shamefast maidens must be shown,
Where they may sport and seem to be unknown.
Then came Corinna in a long loose gown,
Her white neck hid with tresses hanging down,
Resembling fair Semiramis going to bed,
Or Lais of a thousand wooers sped.
I snatched her gown; being thin, the harm was small,
Yet strived she to be covered therewithal,
And striving thus as one that would be cast,
Betrayed herself, and yielded at the last.
Stark naked as she stood before mine eye,
Not one wen in her body could I spy.
What arms and shoulders did I touch and see,
How apt her breasts were to be pressed by me!
How smooth a belly under her waist saw I,
How large a leg, and what a lusty thigh!
To leave the rest, all liked me passing well;
I clinged her naked body, down she fell.
Judge you the rest: being tired she bade me kiss;
Jove send me more such afternoons as this.

ELEGIA VI
Ad Janitorem, ut fores sibi aperiat

Unworthy porter, bound in chains full sore,
On movèd hooks set ope the churlish door.
Little I ask, a little entrance make;
The gate half-ope my bent side in will take.

Long love my body to such use makes slender,
And to get out doth like apt members render.
He shows me how unheard to pass the watch,
And guides my feet lest stumbling falls they catch.
But in times past I feared vain shades, and night,
Wond'ring if any walkèd without light.
Love hearing it laughed with his tender mother,
And smiling said, 'Be thou as bold as other.'
Forthwith Love came: no dark night-flying sprite,
Nor hands prepared to slaughter, me affright.
Thee fear I too much, only thee I flatter,
Thy lightning can my life in pieces batter.
Why enviest me? This hostile den unbar,
See how the gates with my tears watered are.
When thou stood'st naked, ready to be beat,
For thee I did thy mistress fair entreat;
But what entreats for thee sometimes took place
(O mischief) now for me obtain small grace.
Gratis thou mayst be free, give like for like,
Night goes away: the door's bar backward strike.
Strike, so again hard chains shall bind thee never,
Nor servile water shalt thou drink for ever.
Hard-hearted porter, dost and wilt not hear?
With stiff oak propped the gate doth still appear.
Such rampired gates besiegèd cities aid,
In midst of peace why art of arms afraid?
Exclud'st a lover, how would'st use a foe?
Strike back the bar, night fast away doth go.
With arms or armèd men I come not guarded,
I am alone, were furious Love discarded.
Although I would, I cannot him cashier
Before I be divided from my gear.
See Love with me, wine moderate in my brain,
And on my hairs a crown of flowers remain.
Who fears these arms? Who will not go to meet them?
Night runs away; with open entrance greet them.
Art careless? Or is 't sleep forbids thee hear,
Giving the winds my words running in thine ear?
Well I remember when I first did hire thee,
Watching till after midnight did not tire thee;
But now perchance thy wench with thee doth rest —
Ah, how thy lot is above my lot blest!

Though it be so, shut me not out therefore;
Night goes away, I pray thee ope the door.
Err we? Or do the turnèd hinges sound,
And opening doors with creaking noise abound?
We err: a strong blast seemed the gates to ope;
Aye me, how high that gale did lift my hope!
If, Boreas, bears Orithyia's rape in mind,
Come break these deaf doors with thy boisterous wind.
Silent the city is: night's dewy host
March fast away; the bar strike from the post,
Or I more stern than fire or sword will turn
And with my brand these gorgeous houses burn.
Night, love, and wine to all extremes persuade;
Night, shameless wine, and love are fearless made.
All have I spent: no threats or prayers move thee;
O harder than the doors thou guard'st I prove thee.
No pretty wench's keeper mayst thou be:
The careful prison is more meet for thee.
Now frosty night her flight begins to take,
And crowing cocks poor souls to work awake;
But thou my crown, from sad hairs ta'en away,
On this hard threshold till the morning lay,
That when my mistress there beholds thee cast,
She may perceive how we the time did waste.
Whate'er thou art, farewell; be like me pained,
Careless, farewell, with my fault not distained!
And farewell cruel posts, rough threshold's block,
And doors conjoined with a hard iron lock!

ELEGIA VII
Ad pacandam amicam, quam verberaverat

Bind fast my hands, they have deservèd chains,
While rage is absent, take some friend the pains;
For rage against my wench moved my rash arm,
My mistress weeps whom my mad hand did harm.
I might have then my parents dear misused,
Or holy gods with cruel strokes abused.
Why, Ajax, master of the seven-fold shield,
Butchered the flocks he found in spacious field,
And he who on his mother venged his sire
Against the Destinies durst sharp darts require.

Could I therefore her comely tresses tear?
Yet was she gracèd with her ruffled hair.
So fair she was, Atalanta she resembled,
Before whose bow th' Arcadian wild beasts trembled;
Such Ariadne was, when she bewails
Her perjured Theseus' flying vows and sails;
So, chaste Minerva, did Cassandra fall,
Deflowered except, within thy temple wall.
That I was mad and barbarous all men cried,
She nothing said, pale fear her tongue had tied;
But secretly her looks with checks did trounce me,
Her tears, she silent, guilty did pronounce me.
Would of mine arms my shoulders had been scanted,
Better I could part of myself have wanted.
To mine own self have I had strength so furious,
And to myself could I be so injurious?
Slaughter and mischief's instruments, no better,
Deservèd chains these cursèd hands shall fetter.
Punished I am, if I a Roman beat;
Over my mistress is my right more great?
Tydides left worst signs of villainy,
He first a goddess struck; another I.
Yet he harmed less; whom I professed to love
I harmed; a foe did Diomedes' anger move.
Go now, thou conqueror, glorious triumphs raise,
Pay vows to Jove, engirt thy hairs with bays,
And let the troops which shall thy chariot follow
'Io, a strong man conquered this wench,' hollow.
Let the sad captive foremost with locks spread,
On her white neck but for hurt cheeks be led;
Meeter it were her lips were blue with kissing,
And on her neck a wanton's mark not missing.
But though I like a swelling flood was driven,
And like a prey unto blind anger given,
Was 't not enough the fearful wench to chide,
Nor thunder in rough threatings' haughty pride,
Nor shamefully her coat pull o'er her crown,
Which to her waist her girdle still kept down?
But cruelly her tresses having rent,
My nails to scratch her lovely cheeks I bent.
Sighing she stood, her bloodless white looks showèd
Like marble from the Parian mountains hewèd;
Her half-dead joints and trembling limbs I saw,

Like poplar leaves blown with a stormy flaw,
Or slender ears with gentle Zephyr shaken,
Or waters' tops with the warm south wind taken.
And down her cheeks the trickling tears did flow
Like water gushing from consuming snow.
Then first I did perceive I had offended,
My blood the tears were that from her descended.
Before her feet thrice prostrate down I fell,
My fearèd hands thrice back she did repel.
But doubt thou not (revenge doth grief appease)
With thy sharp nails upon my face to seize;
Bescratch mine eyes, spare not my locks to break
(Anger will help thy hands though ne'er so weak),
And lest the sad signs of my crime remain,
Put in their place thy kembèd hairs again.

ELEGIA VIII
Execratur lenam, quae puellam suam meretricia arte instituebat

There is—whoe'er will know a bawd aright,
Give ear—there is an old trot, Dipsas hight.
Her name comes from the thing: she being wise
Sees not the morn on rosy horses-rise,
She magic arts and Thessale charms doth know,
And makes large streams back to their fountains flow;
She knows with grass, with threads on wrong wheels spun,
And what with mares' rank humour may be done.
When she will, clouds the darkened heav'n obscure;
When she will, day shines everywhere most pure.
If I have faith, I saw the stars drop blood,
The purple moon with sanguine visage stood.
Her I suspect among night's spirits to fly,
And her old body in birds' plumes to lie.
Fame saith as I suspect, and in her eyes
Two eyeballs shine and double light thence flies.
Great-grandsires from their ancient graves she chides,
And with long charms the solid earth divides.
She draws chaste women to incontinence,
Nor doth her tongue want harmful eloquence.
By chance I heard her talk; these words she said,
While closely hid betwixt two doors I laid:
'Mistress, thou know'st thou hast a blest youth pleased,

He stayed and on thy looks his gazes seized.
And why shouldst not please? None thy face exceeds;
Aye me, thy body hath no worthy weeds.
As thou art fair, would thou wert fortunate!
Wert thou rich, poor should not be my state.
Th' opposèd star of Mars hath done thee harm;
Now Mars is gone, Venus thy side doth warm,
And brings good fortune: a rich lover plants
His love on thee, and can supply thy wants.
Such is his form as may with thine compare,
Would he not buy thee, thou for him shouldst care.'
She blushed. 'Red shame becomes white cheeks, but this,
If feigned, doth well; if true, it doth amiss.
When on thy lap thine eyes thou dost deject,
Each one according to his gifts respect.
Perhaps the Sabines rude, when Tatius reigned,
To yield their love to more than one disdained;
Now Mars doth rage abroad without all pity,
And Venus rules in her Aeneas' city.
Fair women play, she's chaste whom none will have,
Or, but for bashfulness, herself would crave.
Shake off these wrinkles that thy front assault,
Wrinkles in beauty is a grievous fault.
Penelope in bows her youths' strength tried,
Of horn the bow was that approved their side.
Time flying slides hence closely, and deceives us.
And with swift horses the swift year soon leaves us.
Brass shines with use; good garments would be worn;
Houses not dwelt in are with filth forlorn.
Beauty not exercised with age is spent,
Nor one or two men are sufficient.
Many to rob is more sure, and less hateful,
From dog-kept flocks come preys to wolves most grateful.
Behold, what gives the poet but new verses?
And thereof many thousand he rehearses.
The poet's god, arrayed in robes of gold,
Of his gilt harp the well-turned strings doth hold.
Let Homer yield to such as presents bring;
(Trust me) to give, it is a witty thing.
Nor, so thou mayst obtain a wealthy prize,
The vain name of inferior slaves despise.
Nor let the arms of ancient lines beguile thee;
Poor lover, with thy grandsires I exile thee.

Who seeks, for being fair, a night to have,
What he will give, with greater instance crave.
Make a small price, while thou thy nets dost lay,
Lest they should fly; being ta'en, the tyrant play.
Dissemble so, as loved he may be thought,
And take heed lest he gets that love for nought.
Deny him oft; feign now thy head doth ache:
And Isis now will show what scuse to make.
Receive him soon, lest patient use he gain,
Or lest his love oft beaten back should wane.
To beggars shut, to bringers ope thy gate;
Let him within hear barred-out lovers prate.
And as first wronged the wrongèd sometimes banish,
Thy fault with his fault so repulsed will vanish.
But never give a spacious time to ire,
Anger delayed doth oft to hate retire.
And let thine eyes constrainèd learn to weep,
That this or that man may thy cheeks moist keep.
Nor, if thou cozen'st one, dread to forswear,
Venus to mocked men lends a senseless ear.
Servants fit for thy purpose thou must hire,
To teach thy lover what thy thoughts desire.
Let them ask somewhat; many asking little,
Within a while great heaps grow of a tittle.
And sister, nurse, and mother spare him not,
By many hands great wealth is quickly got.
When causes fail thee to require a gift,
By keeping of thy birth make but a shift.
Beware lest he unrivalled loves secure;
Take strife away, love doth not well endure.
On all the bed men's tumbling let him view,
And thy neck with lascivious marks made blue;
Chiefly show him the gifts which others send;
If he gives nothing, let him from thee wend.
When thou hast so much as he gives no more,
Pray him to lend what thou mayst ne'er restore.
Let thy tongue flatter, while thy mind harm works,
Under sweet honey deadly poison lurks.
If this thou dost, to me by long use known,
Nor let my words be with the winds hence blown,
Oft thou wilt say, "live well"; thou wilt pray oft
That my dead bones may in their grave lie soft.'
As thus she spake, my shadow me betrayed,

With much ado my hands I scarcely stayed;
But her blear eyes, bald scalp's thin hoary fleeces,
And rivelled cheeks I would have pulled a-pieces.
The gods send thee no house, a poor old age,
Perpetual thirst, and winter's lasting rage.

ELEGIA IX
Ad Atticum, amantem non oportere desidiosum esse, sicuti nec militem

All lovers war, and Cupid hath his tent,
Attic, all lovers are to war far sent.
What age fits Mars, with Venus doth agree,
'Tis shame for eld in war or love to be.
What years in soldiers captains do require,
Those in their lovers pretty maids desire.
Both of them watch: each on the hard earth sleeps;
His mistress' doors this, that his captain's keeps.
Soldiers must travel far; the wench forth send,
Her valiant lover follows without end.
Mounts, and rain-doubled floods he passeth over,
And treads the deserts snowy heaps do cover.
Going to sea, east winds he doth not chide,
Nor to hoist sail attends fit time and tide.
Who but a soldier or a lover is bold
To suffer storm-mixed snows with night's sharp cold?
One as a spy doth to his enemies go,
The other eyes his rival as his foe.
He cities great, this thresholds lies before;
This breaks town gates, but he his mistress' door.
Oft to invade the sleeping foe 'tis good,
And armed to shed unarmèd people's blood.
So the fierce troops of Thracian Rhesus fell,
And captive horses bade their lord farewell.
Sooth, lovers watch till sleep the husband charms,
Who slumb'ring, they rise up in swelling arms.
The keeper's hands and corps-du-gard to pass,
The soldier's, and poor lover's work e'er was.
Doubtful is war and love: the vanquished rise,
And who thou never think'st should fall, down lies.
Therefore whoe'er love slothfulness doth call,
Let him surcease: love tries wit best of all.
Achilles burned, Briseis being ta'en away;

Trojans, destroy the Greek wealth while you may;
Hector to arms went from his wife's embraces,
And on Andromache his helmet laces.
Great Agamemnon was, men say, amazed,
On Priam's loose-tressed daughter when he gazed.
Mars in the deed the blacksmith's net did stable,
In heaven was never more notorious fable.
Myself was dull and faint, to sloth inclined,
Pleasure and ease had mollified my mind;
A fair maid's care expelled this sluggishness,
And to her tents willed me myself address.
Since mayst thou see me watch and night-wars move:
He that will not grow slothful, let him love.

ELEGIA X
Ad puellam, ne pro amore praemia poscat

Such as the cause was of two husbands' war,
Whom Trojan ships fetched from Europa far;
Such as was Leda, whom the god deluded
In snow-white plumes of a false swan included;
Such as Amymone through the dry fields strayed,
When on her head a water pitcher laid:
Such wert thou, and I feared the bull and eagle,
And whate'er Love made Jove should thee inveigle.
Now all fear with my mind's hot love abates,
No more this beauty mine eyes captivates.
Ask'st why I change? Because thou crav'st reward:
This cause hath thee from pleasing me debarred.
While thou wert plain, I loved thy mind and face,
Now inward faults thy outward form disgrace.
Love is a naked boy, his years sans stain,
And hath no clothes, but open doth remain.
Will you for gain have Cupid sell himself?
He hath no bosom, where to hide base pelf.
Love and Love's son are with fierce arms to odds;
To serve for pay beseems not wanton gods.
The whore stands to be bought for each man's money,
And seeks vile wealth by selling of her coney,
Yet greedy bawd's command she curseth still,
And doth, constrained, what you do of good will.
Take from irrational beasts a precedent;

'Tis shame their wits should be more excellent.
The mare asks not the horse, the cow the bull,
Nor the mild ewe gifts from the ram doth pull;
Only a woman gets spoils from a man,
Farms out herself on nights for what she can,
And lets what both delight, what both desire,
Making her joy according to her hire.
The sport being such as both alike sweet try it,
Why should one sell it and the other buy it?
Why should I lose, and thou gain by the pleasure
Which man and woman reap in equal measure?
Knights of the post of perjuries make sale,
The unjust judge for bribes becomes a stale.
'Tis shame sold tongues the guilty should defend,
Or great wealth from a judgement seat ascend;
'Tis shame to grow rich by bed merchandise,
Or prostitute thy beauty for bad prize.
Thanks worthily are due for things unbought,
For beds ill-hired we are indebted nought.
The hirer payeth all, his rent discharged,
From further duty he rests then enlarged.
Fair dames forbear rewards for nights to crave,
Ill-gotten goods good end will never have.
The Sabine gauntlets were too dearly won,
That unto death did press the holy nun.
The son slew her that forth to meet him went,
And a rich necklace caused that punishment.
Yet think no scorn to ask a wealthy churl;
He wants no gifts into thy lap to hurl.
Take clustered grapes from an o'er-laden vine,
May bounteous loam Alcinous' fruit resign.
Let poor men show their service, faith, and care;
All for their mistress, what they have, prepare.
In verse to praise kind wenches 'tis my part,
And whom I like eternize by mine art.
Garments do wear, jewels and gold do waste,
The fame that verse gives doth for ever last.
To give I love, but to be asked disdain;
Leave asking, and I'll give what I refrain.

ELEGIA XI
Napen alloquitur, ut paratas tabellas ad Corinnam perferat

> In skilful gathering ruffled hairs in order,
> Nape, free-born, whose cunning hath no border,
> Thy service for night's scapes is known commodious,
> And to give signs dull wit to thee is odious.
> Corinna clips me oft by thy persuasion,
> Never to harm me made thy faith evasion.
> Receive these lines, them to thy mistress carry,
> Be sedulous, let no stay cause thee tarry.
> Nor flint nor iron are in thy soft breast,
> But pure simplicity in thee doth rest.
> And 'tis supposed Love's bow hath wounded thee,
> Defend the ensigns of thy war in me.
> If what I do, she asks, say 'hope for night';
> The rest my hand doth in my letters write.
> Time passeth while I speak, give her my writ,
> But see that forthwith she peruseth it.
> I charge thee mark her eyes and front in reading,
> By speechless looks we guess at things succeeding.
> Straight being read, will her to write much back,
> I hate fair paper should writ matter lack.
> Let her make verses, and some blotted letter
> On the last edge, to stay mine eyes the better.
> What need she tire her hand to hold the quill?
> Let this word, 'Come,' alone the tables fill.
> Then with triumphant laurel will I grace them,
> And in the midst of Venus' temple place them,
> Subscribing that to her I consecrate
> My faithful tables, being vile maple late.

ELEGIA XII
Tabellas quas miserat execratur, quod amica noctem negabat

> Bewail my chance: the sad book is returnèd,
> This day denial hath my sport adjournèd.
> Presages are not vain; when she departed,
> Nape by stumbling on the threshold started.
> Going out again, pass forth the door more wisely,
> And somewhat higher bear thy foot precisely.
> Hence, luckless tables, funeral wood, be flying,

And thou the wax stuffed full with notes denying,
Which I think gathered from cold hemlock's flower,
Wherein bad honey Corsic bees did pour.
Yet as if mixed with red lead thou wert ruddy,
That colour rightly did appear so bloody.
As evil wood thrown in the highways lie,
Be broke with wheels of chariots passing by,
And him that hewed you out for needful uses
I'll prove had hands impure with all abuses.
Poor wretches on the tree themselves did strangle;
There sat the hangman for men's necks to angle.
To hoarse screech-owls foul shadows it allows,
Vultures and Furies nestled in the boughs.
To these my love I foolishly committed,
And then with sweet words to my mistress fitted;
More fitly had they wrangling bonds contained,
From barbarous lips of some attorney strained.
Among day-books and bills they had lain better,
In which the merchant wails his bankrupt debtor.
Your name approves you made for such like things,
The number two no good divining brings.
Angry, I pray that rotten age you wracks,
And sluttish white-mould overgrow the wax.

ELEGIA XIII
Ad Auroram, ne properet

      Now o'er the sea from her old love comes she
That draws the day from heaven's cold axle-tree.
Aurora, whither slidest thou? Down again,
And birds for Memnon yearly shall be slain.
Now in her tender arms I sweetly bide,
If ever, now well lies she by my side.
The air is cold, and sleep is sweetest now,
And birds send forth shrill notes from every bough:
Whither runn'st thou, that men and women love not?
Hold in thy rosy horses that they move not.
Ere thou rise, stars teach seamen where to sail,
But when thou comest, they of their courses fail.
Poor travellers, though tired, rise at thy sight,
And soldiers make them ready to the fight.
The painful hind by thee to field is sent,

Slow oxen early in the yoke are pent.
Thou cozen'st boys of sleep, and dost betray them
To pedants that with cruel lashes pay them.
Thou mak'st the surety to the lawyer run,
That with one word hath nigh himself undone.
The lawyer and the client hate thy view,
Both whom thou raisest up to toil anew.
By thy means women of their rest are barred,
Thou set'st their labouring hands to spin and card.
All could I bear; but that the wench should rise
Who can endure, save him with whom none lies?
How oft wished I night would not give thee place,
Nor morning stars shun thy uprising face.
How oft that either wind would break thy coach,
Or steeds might fall, forced with thick clouds' approach.
Whither goest thou, hateful nymph? Memnon the elf
Received his coal-black colour from thyself.
Say that thy love with Cephalus were not known,
Then thinkest thou thy loose life is not shown?
Would Tithon might but talk of thee awhile,
Not one in heaven should be more base and vile.
Thou leav'st his bed because he's faint through age,
And early mount'st thy hateful carriage;
But held'st thou in thine arms some Cephalus,
Then wouldst thou cry, 'Stay night, and run not thus.'
Dost punish me, because years make him wane?
I did not bid thee wed an ancient swain.
The moon sleeps with Endymion every day;
Thou art as fair as she, then kiss and play.
Jove, that thou shouldst not haste but wait his leisure,
Made two nights one to finish up his pleasure.
I chid no more; she blushed, and therefore heard me,
Yet lingered not the day, but morning scared me.

ELEGIA XIV
Puellam consolatur cui prae nimia cura comae deciderant

'Leave colouring thy tresses,' I did cry;
Now hast thou left no hairs at all to dye.
But what had been more fair had they been kept?
Beyond thy robes thy dangling locks had swept.
Fear'dst thou to dress them being fine and thin,

Like to the silk the curious Seres spin,
Or threads which spider's slender foot draws out,
Fast'ning her light web some old beam about?
Not black, nor golden were they to our view,
Yet although neither, mixed of either's hue,
Such as in hilly Ida's wat'ry plains,
The cedar tall spoiled of his bark retains.
And they were apt to curl a hundred ways,
And did to thee no cause of dolour raise.
Nor hath the needle, or the comb's teeth reft them,
The maid that kembed them ever safely left them.
Oft was she dressed before mine eyes, yet never,
Snatching the comb to beat the wench, out drave her.
Oft in the morn, her hairs not yet digested,
Half-sleeping on a purple bed she rested;
Yet seemly, like a Thracian bacchanal,
That tired doth rashly on the green grass fall.
When they were slender, and like downy moss,
Thy troubled hairs, alas, endured great loss.
How patiently hot irons they did take,
In crooked trammels crispy curls to make.
I cried, ''Tis sin, 'tis sin, these hairs to burn,
They well become thee, then to spare them turn.
Far off be force, no fire to them may reach,
Thy very hairs will the hot bodkin teach.'
Lost are the goodly locks, which from their crown
Phoebus and Bacchus wished were hanging down.
Such were they as Diana painted stands
All naked holding in her wave-moist hands.
Why dost thy ill-kembed tresses' loss lament?
Why in thy glass dost look being discontent?
Be not to see with wonted eyes inclined;
To please thyself, thyself put out of mind.
No charmèd herbs of any harlot scathed thee,
No faithless witch in Thessale waters bathed thee.
No sickness harmed thee (far be that away!),
No envious tongue wrought thy thick locks decay.
By thine own hand and fault thy hurt doth grow,
Thou mad'st thy head with compound poison flow.
Now Germany shall captive hair-tires send thee,
And vanquished people curious dressings lend thee,
Which some admiring, O thou oft wilt blush,
And say, 'He likes me for my borrowed bush,

Praising for me some unknown Guelder dame,
But I remember when it was my fame.'
Alas she almost weeps, and her white cheeks,
Dyed red with shame, to hide from shame she seeks.
She holds, and views her old locks in her lap;
Aye me, rare gifts unworthy such a hap.
Cheer up thyself, thy loss thou mayst repair,
And be hereafter seen with native hair.

ELEGIA XV
Ad invidos, quod fama poetarum sit perennis

Envy, why carp'st thou my time is spent so ill,
And term'st my works fruits of an idle quill?
Or that unlike the line from whence I sprung,
War's rusty honours are refused, being young?
Nor that I study not the brawling laws,
Nor set my voice to sale in every cause?
Thy scope is mortal, mine eternal fame,
That all the world may ever chant my name.
Homer shall live while Tenedos stands and Ide,
Or into sea swift Simois doth slide.
Ascraeus lives while grapes with new wine swell,
Or men with crooked sickles corn down fell.
The world shall of Callimachus ever speak;
His art excelled, although his wit was weak.
For ever lasts high Sophocles' proud vein,
With sun and moon Aratus shall remain.
While bondmen cheat, fathers be hard, bawds whorish,
And strumpets flatter, shall Menander flourish.
Rude Ennius, and Plautus full of wit,
Are both in fame's eternal legend writ.
What age of Varro's name shall not be told,
And Jason's Argos and the fleece of gold?
Lofty Lucretius shall live that hour
That nature shall dissolve this earthly bower.
Aeneas' war, and Tityrus shall be read,
While Rome of all the conquered world is head.
Till Cupid's bow and fiery shafts be broken,
Thy verses, sweet Tibullus, shall be spoken.
And Gallus shall be known from east to west;
So shall Lycoris whom he lovèd best.

Therefore when flint and iron wear away,
Verse is immortal, and shall ne'er decay.
To verse let kings give place, and kingly shows,
And banks o'er which gold-bearing Tagus flows.
Let base-conceited wits admire vile things,
Fair Phoebus lead me to the Muses' springs.
About my head be quivering myrtle wound,
And in sad lovers' heads let me be found.
The living, not the dead, can envy bite,
For after death all men receive their right.
Then though death rakes my bones in funeral fire,
I'll live, and as he pulls me down mount higher.

Ovid's Elegies: Book Two

ELEGIA I
Quod pro gigantomachia amores scribere sit coactus

I, Ovid, poet of my wantonness,
Born at Peligny, to write more address.
So Cupid wills; far hence be the severe:
You are unapt my looser lines to hear.
Let maids whom hot desire to husbands lead,
And rude boys touched with unknown love, me read,
That some youth hurt as I am with Love's bow
His own flame's best acquainted signs may know,
And long admiring say, 'By what means learned
Hath this same poet my sad chance discerned?'
I durst the great celestial battles tell,
Hundred-hand Gyges, and had done it well,
With earth's revenge, and how Olympus' top
High Ossa bore, Mount Pelion up to prop.
Jove and Jove's thunderbolts I had in hand,
Which for his heaven fell on the giants' band.
My wench her door shut, Jove's affairs I left,
Even Jove himself out of my wit was reft.
Pardon me, Jove, thy weapons aid me nought,
Her shut gates greater lightning than thine brought.
Toys and light elegies, my darts, I took,
Quickly soft words hard doors wide open strook.
Verses reduce the hornèd bloody moon,
And call the sun's white horses back at noon.
Snakes leap by verse from caves of broken mountains,

And turnèd streams run backward to their fountains.
Verses ope doors; and locks put in the post,
Although of oak, to yield to verse's boast.
What helps it me of fierce Achill to sing?
What good to me will either Ajax bring?
Or he who warred and wandered twenty year?
Or woeful Hector, whom wild jades did tear?
But when I praise a pretty wench's face,
She in requital doth me oft embrace.
A great reward: heroes, O famous names,
Farewell; your favour nought my mind inflames.
Wenches, apply your fair looks to my verse,
Which golden Love doth unto me rehearse.

ELEGIA II
Ad Bagoum, ut custodiam puellae sibi commissae laxiorem habeat

Bagous, whose care doth thy mistress bridle,
While I speak some few yet fit words, be idle.
I saw the damsel walking yesterday
There where the porch doth Danaus' fact display.
She pleased me soon, I sent, and did her woo,
Her trembling hand writ back she might not do.
And asking why, this answer she redoubled,
Because thy care too much thy mistress troubled.
Keeper, if thou be wise, cease hate to cherish;
Believe me, whom we fear, we wish to perish.
Nor is her husband wise; what needs defence,
When unprotected there is no expense?
But furiously he follow his love's fire,
And think her chaste whom many do desire.
Stol'n liberty she may by thee obtain,
Which giving her, she may give thee again.
Wilt thou her fault learn, she may make thee tremble;
Fear to be guilty, then thou mayst dissemble.
Think when she reads, her mother letters sent her;
Let him go forth known, that unknown did enter;
Let him go see her though she do not languish,
And then report her sick and full of anguish.
If long she stays, to think the time more short,
Lay down thy forehead in thy lap to snort.
Enquire not what with Isis may be done,

Nor fear lest she to the theatres run.
Knowing her scapes, thine honour shall increase,
And what less labour than to hold thy peace?
Let him please, haunt the house, be kindly used,
Enjoy the wench, let all else be refused.
Vain causes feign of him, the true to hide,
And what she likes let both hold ratified.
When most her husband bends the brows and frowns,
His fawning wench with her desire he crowns.
But yet sometimes to chide thee let her fall
Counterfeit tears, and thee lewd hangman call.
Object thou then what she may well excuse,
To stain all faith in truth, by false crimes' use.
Of wealth and honour so shall grow thy heap;
Do this and soon thou shalt thy freedom reap.
On tell-tales' necks thou seest the link-knit chains,
The filthy prison faithless breasts restrains.
Water in waters, and fruit flying touch
Tantalus seeks, his long tongue's gain is such;
While Juno's watchman Io too much eyed,
Him timeless death took, she was deified.
I saw one's legs with fetters black and blue,
By whom the husband his wife's incest knew.
More he deserved; to both great harm he framed;
The man did grieve, the woman was defamed.
Trust me, all husbands for such faults are sad,
Nor make they any man that hear them glad.
If he loves not, deaf ears thou dost importune;
Or if he loves, thy tale breeds his misfortune.
Nor is it easily proved, though manifest,
She safe by favour of her judge doth rest.
Though himself see, he'll credit her denial,
Condemn his eyes, and say there is no trial.
Spying his mistress' tears, he will lament
And say, 'This blab shall suffer punishment.'
Why fight'st 'gainst odds? To thee, being cast, do hap
Sharp stripes; she sitteth in the judge's lap.
To meet for poison or vile facts we crave not,
My hands an unsheathed shining weapon have not.
We seek that, through thee, safely love we may;
What can be easier than the thing we pray?

ELEGIA III
Ad Eunuchum servantem dominam

> Aye me, a eunuch keeps my mistress chaste,
> That cannot Venus' mutual pleasure taste.
> Who first deprived young boys of their best part,
> With selfsame wounds he gave he ought to smart.
> To kind requests thou wouldst more gentle prove,
> If ever wench had made lukewarm thy love:
> Thou wert not born to ride, or arms to bear,
> Thy hands agree not with the warlike spear.
> Men handle those; all manly hopes resign,
> Thy mistress' ensigns must be likewise thine.
> Please her, her hate makes others thee abhor;
> If she discards thee, what use serv'st thou for?
> Good form there is, years apt to play together,
> Unmeet is beauty without use to wither.
> She may deceive thee, though thou her protect,
> What two determine never wants effect.
> Our prayers move thee to assist our drift,
> While thou hast time yet to bestow that gift.

ELEGIA IV
Quod amet mulieres, cuiuscunque formae sint

> I mean not to defend the scapes of any,
> Or justify my vices being many.
> For I confess, if that might merit favour,
> Here I display my lewd and loose behaviour.
> I loathe, yet after that I loathe I run;
> O how the burden irks, that we should shun.
> I cannot rule myself, but where love please
> Am driven like a ship upon rough seas.
> No one face likes me best, all faces move,
> A hundred reasons make me ever love.
> If any eye me with a modest look,
> I burn, and by that blushful glance am took.
> And she that's coy I like, for being no clown,
> Methinks she would be nimble when she's down.
> Though her sour looks a Sabine's brow resemble,
> I think she'll do, but deeply can dissemble.
> If she be learned, then for her skill I crave her;

If not, because she's simple I would have her.
Before Callimachus one prefers me far;
Seeing she likes my books, why should we jar?
Another rails at me, and that I write;
Yet would I lie with her if that I might.
Trips she, it likes me well; plods she, what then?
She would be nimbler, lying with a man.
And when one sweetly sings, then straight I long
To quaver on her lips even in her song.
Or if one touch the lute with art and cunning,
Who would not love those hands for their swift running?
And her I like that with a majesty
Folds up her arms and makes low courtesy.
To leave myself, that am in love with all,
Some one of these might make the chastest fall.
If she be tall, she's like an Amazon,
And therefore fills the bed she lies upon;
If short, she lies the rounder; to say troth,
Both short and long please me, for I love both.
I think what one undecked would be, being dressed;
Is she attired? Then show her graces best.
A white wench thralls me, so doth golden yellow;
And nut-brown girls in doing have no fellow.
If her white neck be shadowed with black hair,
Why, so was Leda's, yet was Leda fair.
Amber-tressed is she? Then on the morn think I;
My love alludes to every history.
A young wench pleaseth, and an old is good:
This for her looks, that for her womanhood.
Nay what is she that any Roman loves
But my ambitious ranging mind approves?

ELEGIA V
Ad amicam corruptam

    No love is so dear (quivered Cupid, fly!)
That my chief wish should be so oft to die.
Minding thy fault, with death I wish to revel;
Alas, a wench is a perpetual evil.
No intercepted lines thy deeds display,
No gifts given secretly thy crime bewray;
O would my proofs as vain might be withstood,

Aye me, poor soul, why is my cause so good?
He's happy, that his love dares boldly credit,
To whom his wench can say, 'I never did it.'
He's cruel, and too much his grief doth favour,
That seeks the conquest by her loose behaviour.
Poor wretch, I saw when thou didst think I slumbered;
Not drunk, your faults on the spilt wine I numbered.
I saw your nodding eyebrows much to speak,
Even from your cheeks part of a voice did break.
Not silent were thine eyes, the board with wine
Was scribbled, and thy fingers writ a line.
I knew your speech (what do not lovers see?)
And words that seemed for certain marks to be.
Now many guests were gone, the feast being done,
The youthful sort to divers pastimes run.
I saw you then unlawful kisses join
(Such with my tongue it likes me to purloin).
None such the sister gives her brother grave,
But such kind wenches let their lovers have.
Phoebus gave not Diana such, 'tis thought,
But Venus often to her Mars such brought.
'What dost?' I cried, 'transport'st thou my delight?
My lordly hands I'll throw upon my right.
Such bliss is only common to us two,
In this sweet good why hath a third to do?'
This, and what grief enforced me say, I said;
A scarlet blush her guilty face arrayed,
Even such as by Aurora hath the sky,
Or maids that their bethrothèd husbands spy;
Such as a rose mixed with a lily breeds,
Or when the moon travails with charmèd steeds,
Or such as, lest long years should turn the dye,
Arachne stains Assyrian ivory.
To these, or some of these, like was her colour,
By chance her beauty never shinèd fuller.
She viewed the earth: the earth to view beseemed her.
She lookèd sad: sad, comely I esteemed her.
Even kembèd as they were, her locks to rend,
And scratch her fair soft cheeks I did intend.
Seeing her face, mine upreared arms descended,
With her own armour was my wench defended.
I that erewhile was fierce, now humbly sue,
Lest with worse kisses she should me endue.

She laughed, and kissed so sweetly as might make
Wrath-kindled Jove away his thunder shake.
I grieve lest others should such good perceive,
And wish hereby them all unknown to leave.
Also much better were they than I tell,
And ever seemed as some new sweet befell.
'Tis ill they pleased so much, for in my lips
Lay her whole tongue hid, mine in hers she dips.
This grieves me not; no joinèd kisses spent
Bewail I only, though I them lament.
Nowhere can they be taught but in the bed;
I know no master of so great hire sped.

ELEGIA VI
In mortem psittaci

The parrot, from east India to me sent,
Is dead; all fowls her exequies frequent!
Go, godly birds, striking your breasts bewail,
And with rough claws your tender cheeks assail.
For woeful hairs let piece-torn plumes abound,
For long shrilled trumpets let your notes resound.
Why, Philomel, dost Tereus' lewdness mourn?
All wasting years have that complaint outworn.
Thy tunes let this rare bird's sad funeral borrow,
Itys is great, but ancient cause of sorrow.
All you whose pinions in the clear air soar,
But most, thou friendly turtle dove, deplore;
Full concord all your lives was you betwixt,
And to the end your constant faith stood fixed.
What Pylades did to Orestes prove,
Such to the parrot was the turtle dove.
But what availed this faith? Her rarest hue?
Or voice that how to change the wild notes knew?
What helps it thou wert given to please my wench?
Birds' hapless glory, death thy life doth quench.
Thou with thy quills mightst make green emeralds dark,
And pass our scarlet of red saffron's mark;
No such voice-feigning bird was on the ground,
Thou spokest thy words so well with stammering sound.
Envy hath rapt thee, no fierce wars thou movedst,
Vain babbling speech and pleasant peace thou lovedst.

Behold how quails among their battles live,
Which do perchance old age unto them give.
A little filled thee, and for love of talk,
Thy mouth to taste of many meats did balk.
Nuts were thy food, and poppy caused thee sleep,
Pure water's moisture thirst away did keep.
The ravenous vulture lives, the puttock hovers
Around the air, the cadess rain discovers,
And crow survives arms-bearing Pallas' hate,
Whose life nine ages scarce bring out of date.
Dead is that speaking image of man's voice,
The parrot given me, the far world's best choice.
The greedy spirits take the best things first,
Supplying their void places with the worst.
Thersites did Protesilaus survive,
And Hector died, his brothers yet alive.
My wench's vows for thee what should I show,
Which stormy south winds into sea did blow?
The seventh day came, none following mightst thou see,
And the Fate's distaff empty stood to thee;
Yet words in thy benumbèd palate rung:
'Farewell, Corinna,' cried thy dying tongue.
Elysium hath a wood of holm-trees black,
Whose earth doth not perpetual green grass lack;
There good birds rest (if we believe things hidden)
Whence unclean fowls are said to be forbidden;
There harmless swans feed all abroad the river,
There lives the Phoenix one alone bird ever,
There Juno's bird displays his gorgeous feather,
And loving doves kiss eagerly together.
The parrot into wood received with these,
Turns all the goodly birds to what she please.
A grave her bones hides; on her corpse' great grave
The little stones these little verses have:
'This tomb approves I pleased my mistress well,
My mouth in speaking did all birds excel.'

ELEGIA VII
Amicae se purgat quod ancillam non amet

Dost me of new crimes always guilty frame?
To overcome, so oft to fight I shame.
If on the marble theatre I look,

One among many is to grieve thee took.
If some fair wench me secretly behold,
Thou arguest she doth secret marks unfold.
If I praise any, thy poor hairs thou tearest;
If blame, dissembling of my fault thou fearest.
If I look well, thou think'st thou dost not move;
If ill, thou say'st I die for others' love.
Would I were culpable of some offence,
They that deserve pain, bear 't with patience.
Now rash accusing, and thy vain belief,
Forbid thine anger to procure my grief.
Lo, how the miserable great-eared ass,
Dulled with much beating, slowly forth doth pass.
Behold Cypassis, wont to dress thy head,
Is charged to violate her mistress' bed.
The gods from this sin rid me of suspicion,
To like a base wench of despised condition.
With Venus' game who will a servant grace?
Or any back made rough with stripes embrace?
Add she was diligent thy locks to braid,
And for her skill to thee a grateful maid,
Should I solicit her that is so just,
To take repulse, and cause her show my lust?
I swear by Venus, and the winged boy's bow,
Myself unguilty of this crime I know.

ELEGIA VIII
Ad Cypassim ancillam Corinnae

Cypassis, that a thousand ways trim'st hair,
Worthy to kemb none but a goddess fair,
Our pleasant scapes show thee no clown to be,
Apt to thy mistress, but more apt to me.
Who that our bodies were compressed bewrayed?
Whence knows Corinna that with thee I played?
Yet blushed I not, nor used I any saying
That might be urged to witness our false playing.
What if a man with bondwomen offend,
To prove him foolish did I e'er contend?
Achilles burned with face of captive Briseis,
Great Agamemnon loved his servant Chryseis.
Greater than these myself I not esteem;
What gracèd kings, in me no shame I deem.

But when on thee her angry eyes did rush,
In both thy cheeks she did perceive thee blush.
But being present, might that work the best,
By Venus' deity how did I protest!
Thou, goddess, dost command a warm south blast
My false oaths in Carpathian seas to cast.
For which good turn my sweet reward repay,
Let me lie with thee, brown Cypass, today.
Ungrate, why feignest new fears, and dost refuse?
Well mayst thou one thing for thy mistress use.
If thou deniest, fool, I'll our deeds express,
And as a traitor mine own fault confess,
Telling thy mistress where I was with thee,
How oft, and by what means we did agree.

ELEGIA IX
Ad Cupidinem

      O Cupid, that dost never cease my smart,
O boy, that liest so slothful in my heart,
Why me that always was thy soldier found,
Dost harm, and in thy tents why dost me wound?
Why burns thy brand, why strikes thy bow thy friends?
More glory by thy vanquished foes ascends.
Did not Pelides whom his spear did grieve,
Being required, with speedy help relieve?
Hunters leave taken beasts, pursue the chase,
And than things found do ever further pace.
We people wholly given thee feel thine arms,
Thy dull hand stays thy striving enemies' harms.
Dost joy to have thy hookèd arrows shaked
In naked bones? Love hath my bones left naked.
So many men and maidens without love!
Hence with great laud thou mayst a triumph move.
Rome, if her strength the huge world had not filled,
With strawy cabins now her courts should build.
The weary soldier hath the conquered fields,
His sword laid by, safe, though rude places yields.
The dock inharbours ships drawn from the floods,
Horse freed from service range abroad the woods.
And time it was for me to live in quiet,
That have so oft served pretty wenches' diet.

Yet should I curse a god, if he but said,
'Live without love,' so sweet ill is a maid.
For when my loathing it of heat deprives me,
I know not whither my mind's whirlwind drives me.
Even as a headstrong courser bears away
His rider vainly striving him to stay, ·
Or as a sudden gale thrusts into sea
The haven-touching bark now near the lea,
So wavering Cupid brings me back amain,
And purple Love resumes his darts again.
Strike, boy, I offer thee my naked breast,
Here thou hast strength, here thy right hand doth rest.
Here of themselves thy shafts come, as if shot;
Better than I their quiver knows them not.
Hapless is he that all the night lies quiet,
And slumb'ring, thinks himself much blessèd by it.
Fool, what is sleep but image of cold death?
Long shalt thou rest when Fates expire thy breath.
But me let crafty damsel's words deceive,
Great joys by hope I inly shall conceive.
Now let her flatter me, now chide me hard,
Let her enjoy me oft, oft be debarred.
Cupid, by thee Mars in great doubt doth trample,
And thy stepfather fights by thy example.
Light art thou, and more windy than thy wings;
Joys with uncertain faith thou takest and brings.
Yet, Love, if thou with thy fair mother hear,
Within my breast no desert empire bear;
Subdue the wand'ring wenches to thy reign,
So of both people shalt thou homage gain.

ELEGIA X

Ad Graecinum quod eodem tempore duas amet

Graecinus (well I wot) thou told'st me once
I could not be in love with two at once.
By thee deceived, by thee surprised am I,
For now I love two women equally.
Both are well favoured, both rich in array,
Which is the loveliest it is hard to say.
This seems the fairest, so doth that to me,
And this doth please me most, and so doth she.

Even as a boat tossed by contrary wind,
So with this love and that, wavers my mind.
Venus, why doublest thou my endless smart?
Was not one wench enough to grieve my heart?
Why add'st thou stars to heaven, leaves to green woods,
And to the vast deep sea fresh water floods?
Yet this is better far than lie alone;
Let such as be mine enemies have none.
Yea, let my foes sleep in an empty bed,
And in the midst their bodies largely spread.
But may soft love rouse up my drowsy eyes,
And from my mistress' bosom let me rise.
Let one wench cloy me with sweet love's delight,
If one can do 't, if not, two every night.
Though I am slender, I have store of pith,
Nor want I strength, but weight, to press her with.
Pleasure adds fuel to my lustful fire,
I pay them home with that they most desire.
Oft have I spent the night in wantonness,
And in the morn been lively ne'er the less.
He's happy who love's mutual skirmish slays,
And to the gods for that death Ovid prays.
Let soldiers chase their enemies amain,
And with their blood eternal honour gain;
Let merchants seek wealth with perjurèd lips,
Being wracked, carouse the sea tired by their ships;
But when I die, would I might droop with doing,
And in the midst thereof, set my soul going,
That at my funerals some may weeping cry,
'Even as he led his life, so did he die.'

ELEGIA XI
Ad amicam navigantem

The lofty pine, from high Mount Pelion raught,
Ill ways by rough seas wond'ring waves first taught,
Which rashly 'twixt the sharp rocks in the deep
Carried the famous golden-fleecèd sheep.
O would that no oars might in seas have sunk,
The Argos wracked had deadly waters drunk.
Lo, country gods and known bed to forsake
Corinna means, and dangerous ways to take.

For thee the east and west winds make me pale,
With icy Boreas, and the southern gale.
Thou shalt admire no woods or cities there,
The unjust seas all bluish do appear.
The ocean hath no painted stones or shells,
The sucking shore with their abundance swells.
Maids, on the shore with marble-white feet tread,
So far 'tis safe; but to go farther dread.
Let others tell how winds fierce battles wage,
How Scylla's and Charybdis' waters rage,
And with what rocks the feared Cerannia threat,
In what gulf either Syrtes have their seat.
Let others tell this, and what each one speaks
Believe; no tempest the believer wreaks.
Too late you look back, when with anchors weighed,
The crooked bark hath her swift sails displayed.
The careful shipman now fears angry gusts,
And with the waters sees death near him thrusts.
But if that Triton toss the troubled flood,
In all thy face will be no crimson blood.
Then wilt thou Leda's noble twin-stars pray,
And 'he is happy whom the earth holds' say.
It is more safe to sleep, to read a book,
The Thracian harp with cunning to have strook;
But if my words with wingèd storms hence slip,
Yet, Galatea, favour thou her ship.
The loss of such a wench much blame will gather,
Both to the sea-nymphs and the sea-nymphs' father.
Go, minding to return with prosperous wind,
Whose blast may hither strongly be inclined,
Let Nereus bend the waves unto this shore,
Hither the winds blow, here the spring-tide roar.
Request mild Zephyr's help for thy avail,
And with thy hand assist the swelling sail.
I from the shore thy known ship first will see,
And say it brings her that preserveth me.
I'll clip and kiss thee with all contentation,
For thy return shall fall the vowed oblation,
And in the form of beds we'll strew soft sand,
Each little hill shall for a table stand:
There wine being filled, thou many things shalt tell,
How almost wracked thy ship in main seas fell,
And hasting to me, neither darksome night,

Nor violent south winds did thee aught affright.
I'll think all true, though it be feignèd matter;
Mine own desires why should myself not flatter?
Let the bright day-star cause in heaven this day be,
To bring that happy time so soon as may be.

ELEGIA XII
Exultat, quod amica potitus sit

About my temples go, triumphant bays!
Conquered Corinna in my bosom lays,
She whom her husband, guard, and gate, as foes,
Lest art should win her, firmly did enclose.
That victory doth chiefly triumph merit,
Which without bloodshed doth the prey inherit.
No little ditchèd towns, no lowly walls,
But to my share a captive damsel falls.
When Troy by ten years' battle tumbled down,
With the Atrides many gained renown:
But I no partner of my glory brook,
Nor can another say his help I took.
I, guide and soldier, won the field and wear her,
I was both horseman, footman, standard-bearer.
Nor in my act hath fortune mingled chance;
O care-got triumph, hitherwards advance!
Nor is my war's cause new; but for a queen
Europe and Asia in firm peace had been.
The Lapiths and the Centaurs, for a woman,
To cruel arms their drunken selves did summon.
A woman forced the Trojans new to enter
Wars, just Latinus, in thy kingdom's centre;
A woman against late-built Rome did send
The Sabine fathers, who sharp wars intend.
I saw how bulls for a white heifer strive,
She looking on them did more courage give.
And me with many, but yet me without murther,
Cupid commands to move his ensigns further.

ELEGIA XIII
Ad Isidem, ut parientem Corinnam iuvet

While rashly her womb's burden she casts out,
Weary Corinna hath her life in doubt.
She secretly with me such harm attempted,
Angry I was, but fear my wrath exempted.
But she conceived of me; or I am sure
I oft have done what might as much procure.
Thou that frequents Canopus' pleasant fields,
Memphis, and Pharos that sweet date trees yields,
And where swift Nile in his large channel skipping,
By seven huge mouths into the sea is slipping,
By feared Anubis' visage I thee pray,
So in thy temples shall Osiris stay,
And the dull snake about thy off'rings creep,
And in thy pomp horned Apis with thee keep:
Turn thy looks hither, and in one spare twain:
Thou givest my mistress life, she mine again.
She oft hath served thee upon certain days,
Where the French rout engirt themselves with bays.
On labouring women thou dost pity take,
Whose bodies with their heavy burdens ache.
My wench, Lucina, I entreat thee favour;
Worthy she is, thou shouldst in mercy save her.
In white, with incense I'll thine altars greet,
Myself will bring vowed gifts before thy feet,
Subscribing, 'Naso with Corinna saved.'
Do but deserve gifts with this title graved.
But if in so great fear I may advise thee,
To have this skirmish fought, let it suffice thee.

ELEGIA XIV
In amicam, quod abortivum ipsa fecerit

What helps it woman to be free from war,
Nor, being armed, fierce troops to follow far,
If without battle self-wrought wounds annoy them,
And their own privy-weaponed hands destroy them?

Who unborn infants first to slay invented,
Deserved thereby with death to be tormented.
Because thy belly should rough wrinkles lack,
Wilt thou thy womb-inclosèd offspring wrack?
Had ancient mothers this vile custom cherished,
All human kind by their default had perished;
Or stones, our stock's original, should be hurled
Again by some in this unpeopled world.
Who should have Priam's wealthy substance won,
If wat'ry Thetis had her child fordone?
In swelling womb her twins had Ilia killed,
He had not been that conquering Rome did build.
Had Venus spoiled her belly's Trojan fruit,
The earth of Caesars had been destitute.
Thou also, that wert born fair, hadst decayed,
If such a work thy mother had assayed.
Myself, that better die with loving may,
Had seen, my mother killing me, no day.
Why takest increasing grapes from vine-trees full?
With cruel hand why dost green apples pull?
Fruits ripe will fall, let springing things increase,
Life is no light price of a small surcease.
Why with hid irons are your bowels torn?
And why dire poison give you babes unborn?
At Colchis stained with children's blood men rail,
And mother-murdered Itys thee bewail;
Both unkind parents, but for causes sad,
Their wedlock's pledges venged their husbands bad.
What Tereus, what Jason you provokes
To plague your bodies with such harmful strokes?
Armenian tigers never did so ill,
Nor dares the lioness her young whelps kill.
But tender damsels do it, though with pain;
Oft dies she that her paunch-wrapt child hath slain;
She dies, and with loose hairs to grave is sent,
And whoe'er see her, worthily lament.
But in the air let these words come to nought,
And my presages of no weight be thought.
Forgive her, gracious gods, this one delict,
And on the next fault punishment inflict.

ELEGIA XV
Ad annulum, quem dono amicae dedit

       Thou ring that shalt my fair girl's finger bind,
Wherein is seen the giver's loving mind,
Be welcome to her, gladly let her take thee,
And her small joint's encircling round hoop make thee.
Fit her so well, as she is fit for me,
And of just compass for her knuckles be.
Blest ring, thou in my mistress' hand shalt lie;
Myself, poor wretch, mine own gifts now envy.
O would that suddenly into my gift
I could myself by secret magic shift!
Then would I wish thee touch my mistress' pap,
And hide thy left hand underneath her lap;
I would get off though strait, and sticking fast,
And in her bosom strangely fall at last.
Then I, that I may seal her privy leaves,
Lest to the wax the hold-fast dry gem cleaves,
Would first my beauteous wench's moist lips touch,
Only I'll sign nought that may grieve me much.
I would not out, might I in one place hit,
But in less compass her small fingers knit.
My life, that I will shame thee, never fear,
Or be a load thou shouldst refuse to bear.
Wear me, when warmest showers thy members wash,
And through the gem let thy lost waters pash.
But seeing thee, I think my thing will swell,
And even the ring perform a man's part well.
Vain things why wish I? Go, small gift from hand,
Let her my faith with thee given understand.

ELEGIA XVI
Ad amicam, ut ad rura sua veniat

      Sulmo, Peligny's third part, me contains,
A small, but wholesome soil with wat'ry veins.
Although the sun to rive the earth incline,
And the Icarian froward dog-star shine,
Pelignian fields with liquid rivers flow,
And on the soft ground fertile green grass grow.

With corn the earth abounds, with vines much more,
And some few pastures Pallas' olives bore.
And by the rising herbs, where clear springs slide,
A grassy turf the moistened earth doth hide.
But absent is my fire: lies I'll tell none,
My heat is here, what moves my heat is gone.
Pollux and Castor might I stand betwixt,
In heaven without thee would I not be fixed.
Upon the cold earth pensive let them lay
That mean to travel some long irksome way,
Or else will maidens, young men's mates, to go
If they determine to persever so.
Then on the rough Alps should I tread aloft,
My hard way with my mistress would seem soft.
With her I durst the Lybian Syrtes break through,
And raging seas in boist'rous south winds plough.
No barking dogs that Scylla's entrails bear,
Nor thy gulfs, crook'd Malea, would I fear;
No flowing waves with drownèd ships forth-pourèd
By cloyed Charybdis, and again devourèd.
But if stern Neptune's windy power prevail,
And waters' force, force helping gods to fail,
With thy white arms upon my shoulders seize,
So sweet a burden I will bear with ease.
The youth oft swimming to his Hero kind,
Had then swum over, but the way was blind.
But without thee, although vine-planted ground
Contains me, though he streams in fields surround,
Though hinds in brooks the running waters bring,
The cool gales shake the tall trees' leafy spring,
Healthful Peligny I esteem nought worth,
Nor do I like the country of my birth.
Scythia, Cilicia, Britain are as good,
And rocks dyed crimson with Prometheus' blood.
Elms love the vines, the vines with elms abide,
Why doth my mistress from me oft divide?
Thou swarest division should not 'twixt us rise,
By me, and by my stars, thy radiant eyes.
Maids' words more vain and light than falling leaves,
Which, as it seems, hence wind and sea bereaves.

If any godly care of me thou hast,
Add deeds unto thy promises at last,
And with swift nags drawing thy little coach
(Their reins let loose), right soon my house approach.
But when she comes, you swelling mounts sink down,
And falling valleys be the smooth ways' crown.

ELEGIA XVII
Quod Corinnae soli sit serviturus

To serve a wench if any think it shame,
He being judge, I am convinced of blame.
Let me be slandered, while my fire she hides,
That Paphos, and the flood-beat Cythera guides.
Would I had been my mistress' gentle prey,
Since some fair one I should of force obey.
Beauty gives heart; Corinna's looks excel;
Aye me, why is it known to her so well?
But by her glass disdainful pride she learns,
Nor she herself, but first trimmed up, discerns.
Not though thy face in all things make thee reign
(O face, most cunning mine eyes to detain!),
Thou oughtst therefore to scorn me for thy mate:
Small things with greater may be copulate.
Love-snared Calypso is supposed to pray
A mortal nymph's refusing lord to stay.
Who doubts with Peleus Thetis did consort,
Egeria with just Numa had good sport,
Venus with Vulcan, though, smith's tools laid by,
With his stump foot he halts ill-favouredly.
This kind of verse is not alike, yet fit,
With shorter numbers the heroic sit.
And thou, my light, accept me howsoever,
Lay in the mid-bed, there be my lawgiver.
My stay no crime, my flight no joy shall breed,
Nor of our love to be ashamed we need.
For great revenues, I good verses have,
And many by me to get glory crave.
I know a wench reports herself Corinne:

What would not she give that fair name to win?
But sundry floods in one bank never go,
Eurotas cold, and poplar-bearing Po.
Nor in my books shall one but thou be writ,
Thou dost alone give matter to my wit.

ELEGIA XVIII
Ad Macrum, quod de amoribus scribat

To tragic verse while thou Achilles train'st,
And new-sworn soldiers' maiden arms retain'st,
We, Macer, sit in Venus' slothful shade,
And tender love hath great things hateful made.
Often at length, my wench depart I bid,
She in my lap sits still as erst she did.
I said, 'It irks me'; half to weeping framed,
'Aye me,' she cries, 'to love why art ashamed?'
Then wreathes about my neck her winding arms,
And thousand kisses gives, that work my harms.
I yield, and back my wit from battles bring,
Domestic acts, and mine own wars to sing.
Yet tragedies and sceptres filled my lines,
But though I apt were for such high designs,
Love laughèd at my cloak, and buskins painted,
And rule so soon with private hands acquainted.
My mistress' deity also drew me fro it,
And Love triumpheth o'er his buskined poet.
What lawful is, or we profess love's art,
(Alas, my precepts turn myself to smart!)
We write, or what Penelope sends Ulysses,
Or Phyllis' tears that her Demophoön misses,
What thankless Jason, Macareus, and Paris,
Phaedra, and Hippolyte may read, my care is,
And what poor Dido with her drawn sword sharp
Doth say, with her that loved the Aonian harp.
As soon as from strange lands Sabinus came,
And writings did from divers places frame,
White-cheeked Penelope knew Ulysses' sign,
The stepdame read Hippolytus' lustless line,
Aeneas to Elisa answer gives,
And Phyllis hath to read, if now she lives.
Jason's sad letter doth Hypsipyle greet,

Sappho her vowed harp lays at Phoebus' feet.
Nor of thee, Macer, that resound'st forth arms,
Is golden love hid in Mars' mid-alarms:
There Paris is, and Helen's crime's record,
With Laodamia, mate to her dead lord.
Unless I err, to these thou more incline
Than wars, and from thy tents wilt come to mine.

ELEGIA XIX
Ad rivalem, cui uxor curae non erat

Fool, if to keep thy wife thou hast no need,
Keep her for me, my more desire to breed.
We scorn things lawful, stol'n sweets we affect,
Cruel is he that loves whom none protect.
Let us both lovers hope and fear alike,
And may repulse place for our wishes strike.
What should I do with fortune that ne'er fails me?
Nothing I love that at all times avails me.
Wily Corinna saw this blemish in me,
And craftily knows by what means to win me.
Ah often, that her hale head ached, she lying,
Willed me, whose slow feet sought delay, be flying;
Ah oft, how much she might, she feigned offence,
And, doing wrong, made show of innocence.
So having vexed she nourished my warm fire,
And was again most apt to my desire.
To please me, what fair terms and sweet words has she!
Great gods, what kisses, and how many gave she!
Thou also, that late took'st mine eyes away,
Oft cozen me, oft being wooed, say nay;
And on thy threshold let me lie dispread,
Suff'ring much cold by hoary night's frost bred.
So shall my love continue many years;
This doth delight me, this my courage cheers.
Fat love, and too much fulsome, me annoys,
Even as sweet meat a glutted stomach cloys.
In brazen tower had not Danae dwelt,
A mother's joy by Jove she had not felt;
While Juno Io keeps, when horns she wore,
Jove liked her better than he did before.
Who covets lawful things takes leaves from woods,

And drinks stol'n waters in surrounding floods.
Her lover let her mock that long will reign;
Aye me, let not my warnings cause my pain!
Whatever haps, by suff'rance harm is done;
What flies I follow, what follows me I shun.
But thou, of thy fair damsel too secure,
Begin to shut thy house at evening sure.
Search at the door who knocks oft in the dark,
In night's deep silence why the ban-dogs bark.
Whether the subtle maid lines brings and carries,
Why she alone in empty bed oft tarries.
Let this care sometimes bite thee to the quick,
That to deceits it may me forward prick.
To steal sands from the shore he loves alife,
That can affect a foolish wittol's wife.
Now I forewarn, unless to keep her stronger
Thou dost begin, she shall be mine no longer.
Long have I borne much, hoping time would beat thee
To guard her well, that well I might entreat thee.
Thou suffer'st what no husband can endure,
But of my love it will an end procure.
Shall I, poor soul, be never interdicted,
Nor never with night's sharp revenge afflicted?
In sleeping shall I fearless draw my breath?
Wilt nothing do, why I should wish thy death?
Can I but loathe a husband grown a bawd?
By thy default thou dost our joys defraud.
Some other seek that may in patience strive with thee;
To pleasure me, forbid me to corrive with thee.

Ovid's Elegies: Book Three

ELEGIA I
Deliberatio poetae, utrum elegos pergat scribere an potius tragedias

> An old wood stands uncut, of long years' space,
> 'Tis credible some godhead haunts the place.
> In midst thereof a stone-paved sacred spring,
> Where round about small birds mostly sweetly sing.
> Here while I walk, hid close in shady grove,
> To find what work my muse might move, I strove.
> Elegia came with hairs perfumèd sweet,
> And one, I think, was longer of her feet;
> A decent form, thin robe, a lover's look,
> By her foot's blemish greater grace she took.
> Then with huge steps came violent Tragedy:
> Stern was her front, her cloak on ground did lie;
> Her left hand held abroad a regal sceptre,
> The Lydian buskin in fit paces kept her.
> And first she said, 'When will thy love be spent,
> O poet careless of thy argument?
> Wine-bibbing banquets tell thy naughtiness,
> Each cross-way's corner doth as much express.
> Oft some points at the prophet passing by,
> And, "This is he whom fierce love burns," they cry.
> A laughing-stock thou art to all the city,
> While without shame thou sing'st thy lewdness' ditty.
> 'Tis time to move grave things in lofty style,

Long hast thou loitered; greater works compile.
The subject hides thy wit; men's acts resound;
This thou wilt say to be a worthy ground.
Thy muse hath played what may mild girls content,
And by those numbers is thy first youth spent.
Now give the Roman Tragedy a name,
To fill my laws thy wanton spirit frame.'
This said, she moved her buskins gaily varnished,
And seven times shook her head with thick locks garnished.
The other smiled (I wot) with wanton eyes;
Err I? Or myrtle in her right hand lies.
'With lofty words, stout Tragedy,' she said,
'Why tread'st me down? Art thou aye gravely played?
Thou deign'st unequal lines should thee rehearse;
Thou fight'st against me using mine own verse;
Thy lofty style with mine I not compare,
Small doors unfitting for large houses are.
Light am I, and with me, my care, light Love,
Not stronger am I than the thing I move.
Venus without me should be rustical;
This goddess' company doth to me befall.
What gate thy stately words cannot unlock,
My flatt'ring speeches soon wide open knock.
And I deserve more than thou canst in verity,
By suff'ring much not borne by thy severity.
By me Corinna learns, cozening her guard,
To get the door with little noise unbarred;
And slipped from bed, clothed in a loose nightgown,
To move her feet unheard in setting down.
Ah, how oft on hard doors hung I engraved,
From no man's reading fearing to be saved!
But till the keeper went forth, I forget not,
The maid to hide me in her bosom let not.
What gift with me was on her birthday sent,
But cruelly by her was drowned and rent.
First of thy mind the happy seeds I knew,
Thou hast my gift, which she would from thee sue.'
She left; I said, 'You both I must beseech,
To empty air may go my fearful speech.
With sceptres and high buskins th' one would dress me,
So through the world should bright renown express me.
The other gives my love a conquering name;
Come therefore, and to long verse shorter frame.

Grant, Tragedy, thy poet time's least tittle,
Thy labour ever lasts, she asks but little.'
She gave me leave, soft loves in time make haste,
Some greater work will urge me on at last.

ELEGIA II
Ad amicam cursum equorum spectantem

      I sit not here the noble horse to see,
Yet whom thou favour'st, pray may conqueror be.
To sit and talk with thee I hither came,
That thou mayst know with love thou mak'st me flame.
Thou view'st the course, I thee: let either heed
What please them, and their eyes let either feed.
What horse-driver thou favour'st most is best,
Because on him thy care doth hap to rest.
Such chance let me have: I would bravely run,
On swift steeds mounted till the race were done.
Now would I slack the reins, now lash their hide,
With wheels bent inward now the ring-turn ride;
In running if I see thee, I shall stay,
And from my hands the reins will slip away.
Ah, Pelops from his coach was almost felled,
Hippodamia's looks while he beheld,
Yet he attained by her support to have her:
Let us all conquer by our mistress' favour.
In vain, why fly'st back? Force conjoins us now:
The place's laws this benefit allow.
But spare my wench, thou at her right hand seated,
By thy side's touching ill she is entreated.
And sit thou rounder, that behind us see;
For shame press not her back with thy hard knee.
But on the ground thy clothes too loosely lie;
Gather them up, or lift them, Io, will I.
Envious garments so good legs to hide!
The more thou look'st, the more the gown envied.
Swift Atalanta's flying legs, like these,
Wish in his hands grasped did Hippomenes.
Coat-tucked Diana's legs are painted like them,
When strong wild beasts she stronger hunts to strike them.
Ere these were seen, I burned; what will these do?
Flames into flame, floods thou pour'st seas into.

By these I judge delight me may the rest,
Which lie hid under her thin veil suppressed.
Yet in the meantime wilt small winds bestow,
That from thy fan, moved by my hand, may blow?
Or is my heat of mind, not of the sky?
Is 't women's love my captive breast doth fry?
While thus I speak, black dust her white robes ray;
Foul dust, from her fair body go away.
Now comes the pomp; themselves let all men cheer:
The shout is nigh, the golden pomp comes here.
First, Victory is brought with large spread wing:
Goddess, come here, make my love conquering.
Applaud you Neptune, that dare trust his wave,
The sea I use not: me my earth must have.
Soldier, applaud thy Mars: no wars we move,
Peace pleaseth me, and in mid-peace is love.
With augurs Phoebus, Phoebe with hunters stands,
To thee, Minerva, turn the craftsmen's hands;
Ceres and Bacchus countrymen adore,
Champions please Pollux, Castor loves horsemen more;
Thee, gentle Venus, and the boy that flies
We praise; great goddess, aid my enterprise.
Let my new mistress grant to be belovèd;
She becked, and prosperous signs gave as she movèd.
What Venus promised, promise thou we pray;
Greater than her, by her leave, th' art, I'll say.
The gods and their rich pomp witness with me,
For evermore thou shalt my mistress be.
Thy legs hang down, thou mayst, if that be best,
Awhile thy tiptoes on the footstool rest.
Now greatest spectacles the praetor sends,
Four-chariot horses from the lists' even ends.
I see whom thou affectest: he shall subdue;
The horses seem as thy desire they knew.
Alas, he runs too far about the ring;
What dost? Thy wagon in less compass bring.
What dost, unhappy? Her good wishes fade,
Let with strong hand the rein to bend be made.
One slow we favour; Romans, him revoke,
And each give signs by casting up his cloak.
They call him back; lest their gowns toss thy hair,
To hide thee in my bosom straight repair.
But now again the barriers open lie,

And forth the gay troops on swift horses fly.
At least now conquer, and outrun the rest;
My mistress' wish confirm with my request.
My mistress hath her wish; my wish remain:
He holds the palm, my palm is yet to gain.
She smiled, and with quick eyes behight some grace:
Pay it not here, but in another place.

ELEGIA III
De amica, quae periuraverat

What, are there gods? Herself she hath forswore,
And yet remains the face she had before.
How long her locks were, ere her oath she took,
So long they be since she her faith forsook.
Fair white with rose red was before commixed;
Now shine her looks pure white and red betwixt.
Her foot was small: her foot's form is most fit;
Comely tall was she: comely tall she's yet.
Sharp eyes she had: radiant like stars they be,
By which she perjured oft hath lied to me.
In sooth th' eternal powers grant maids' society
Falsely to swear, their beauty hath some deity.
By her eyes, I remember, late she swore,
And by mine eyes, and mine were painèd sore.
Say, gods: if she unpunished you deceive,
For other's faults why do I loss receive?
But did you not so envy Cepheus' daughter,
For her ill-beauteous mother judged to slaughter?
'Tis not enough she shakes your record off,
And, unrevenged, mocked gods with me doth scoff.
But by my pain to purge her perjuries,
Cozened, I am the cozener's sacrifice.
God is a name, no substance, feared in vain,
And doth the world in fond belief detain,
Or if there be a God, he loves fine wenches,
And all things too much in their sole power drenches.
Mars girts his deadly sword on for my harm;
Pallas' lance strikes me with unconquered arm;
At me Apollo bends his pliant bow;
At me Jove's right hand lightning hath to throw.
The wrongèd gods dread fair ones to offend,

And fear those, that to fear them least intend.
Who now will care the altars to perfume?
Tut, men should not their courage so consume.
Jove throws down woods and castles with his fire,
But bids his darts from perjured girls retire.
Poor Semele, among so many burned,
Her own request to her own torment turned;
But when her lover came, had she drawn back,
The father's thigh should unborn Bacchus lack.
Why grieve I? And of heaven reproaches pen?
The gods have eyes and breasts as well as men.
Were I a god, I should give women leave
With lying lips my godhead to deceive.
Myself would swear the wenches true did swear,
And I would be none of the gods severe.
But yet their gift more moderately use,
Or in mine eyes, good wench, no pain transfuse.

ELEGIA IV
Ad virum servantem coniugem

Rude man, 'tis vain thy damsel to commend
To keeper's trust: their wits should them defend.
Who, without fear, is chaste, is chaste in sooth:
Who, because means want, doeth not, she doth.
Though thou her body guard, her mind is stained:
Nor, lest she will, can any be restrained.
Nor canst by watching keep her mind from sin;
All being shut out, th' adulterer is within.
Who may offend, sins least; power to do ill
The fainting seeds of naughtiness doth kill.
Forbear to kindle vice by prohibition,
Sooner shall kindness gain thy will's fruition.
I saw a horse against the bit stiff-necked
Like lightning go, his struggling mouth being checked;
When he perceived the reins let slack, he stayed,
And on his loose mane the loose bridle laid.
How to attain what is denied we think,
Even as the sick desire forbidden drink.
Argus had either way a hundred eyes,
Yet by deceit love did them all surprise;
In stone and iron walls Danae shut,

Came forth a mother, though a maid there put.
Penelope, though no watch looked unto her,
Was not defiled by any gallant wooer.
What's kept, we covet more: the care makes theft;
Few love what others have unguarded left.
Nor doth her face please, but her husband's love;
I know not what men think should thee so move.
She is not chaste that's kept, but a dear whore;
Thy fear is than her body valued more.
Although thou chafe, stol'n pleasure is sweet play;
She pleaseth best, 'I fear' if any say.
A free-born wench no right 'tis up to lock,
So use we women of strange nations' stock.
Because the keeper may come say, 'I did it,'
She must be honest to thy servant's credit.
He is too clownish whom a lewd wife grieves,
And this town's well-known custom not believes,
Where Mars his sons not without fault did breed,
Remus and Romulus, Ilia's twin-born seed.
Cannot a fair one, if not chaste, please thee?
Never can these by any means agree.
Kindly thy mistress use, if thou be wise;
Look gently, and rough husbands' laws despise.
Honour what friends thy wife gives, she'll give many;
Least labour so shall win great grace of any;
So shalt thou go with youths to feast together,
And see at home much that thou ne'er brought'st thither.

ELEGIA V
Ad amnem, dum iter faceret ad amicam

       Flood with reed-grown slime banks, till I be past
Thy waters stay; I to my mistress haste.
Thou hast no bridge, nor boat with ropes to throw,
That may transport me without oars to row.
Thee I have passed, and knew thy stream none such,
When thy wave's brim did scarce my ankles touch.
With snow thawed from the next hill now thou rushest,
And in thy foul deep waters thick thou gushest.
What helps my haste? What to have ta'en small rest?
What day and night to travel in her quest,
If standing here I can by no means get

My foot upon the further bank to set?
Now wish I those wings noble Perseus had,
Bearing the head with dreadful adders clad;
Now wish the chariot, whence corn seeds were found,
First to be thrown upon the untilled ground.
I speak old poets' wonderful inventions,
Ne'er was, nor shall be, what my verse mentions.
Rather, thou large bank-overflowing river,
Slide in thy bounds, so shalt thou run for ever.
Trust me, land-stream, thou shalt no envy lack,
If I a lover be by thee held back.
Great floods ought to assist young men in love,
Great floods the force of it do often prove.
In mid-Bithynia, 'tis said, Inachus
Grew pale, and in cold fords hot lecherous.
Troy had not yet been ten years' siege outstander,
When nymph Neaera rapt thy looks, Scamander.
What, not Alpheus in strange lands to run
Th' Arcadian virgin's constant love hath won?
And Creusa unto Xanthus first affied,
They say Peneus near Phthia's town did hide.
What should I name Aesope, that Thebe loved,
Thebe who mother of five daughters proved?
If, Achelous, I ask where thy horns stand,
Thou say'st, broke with Alcides' angry hand.
Not Calydon, nor Aetolia did please;
One Deianira was more worth than these.
Rich Nile by seven mouths to the vast sea flowing,
Who so well keeps his water's head from knowing,
Is by Evadne thought to take such flame
As his deep whirlpools could not quench the same.
Dry Enipeus, Tyro to embrace,
Fly back his stream charged; the stream charged, gave place.
Nor pass I thee, who hollow rocks down tumbling,
In Tiber's field with wat'ry foam art rumbling,
Whom Ilia pleased, though in her looks grief revelled;
Her cheeks were scratched, her goodly hairs dishevelled.
She, wailing Mars' sin and her uncle's crime,
Strayed barefoot through sole places on a time.
Her from his swift waves the bold flood perceived,
And from the mid-ford his hoarse voice upheaved,
Saying, 'Why sadly tread'st my banks upon,
Ilia, sprung from Idaean Laomedon?

Where's thy attire? Why wand'rest here alone?
To stay thy tresses white veil hast thou none?
Why weep'st, and spoil'st with tears thy wat'ry eyes,
And fiercely knock'st thy breast that open lies?
His heart consists of flint and hardest steel,
That seeing thy tears can any joy then feel.
Fear not: to thee our court stands open wide,
There shalt be loved: Ilia, lay fear aside.
Thou o'er a hundred nymphs or more shalt reign,
For five score nymphs or more our floods contain.
Nor, Roman stock, scorn me so much (I crave)
Gifts than my promise greater thou shalt have.'
This said he: she her modest eyes held down,
Her woeful bosom a warm shower did drown.
Thrice she prepared to fly, thrice she did stay,
By fear deprived of strength to run away.
Yet rending with enragèd thumb her tresses,
Her trembling mouth these unmeet sounds expresses:
'O would in my forefathers' tomb deep laid
My bones had been, while yet I was a maid.
Why being a vestal am I wooed to wed,
Deflowered and stainèd in unlawful bed?
Why stay I? Men point at me for a whore,
Shame, that should make be blush, I have no more.'
This said, her coat hoodwinked her fearful eyes,
And into water desperately she flies.
'Tis said the slippery stream held up her breast,
And kindly gave her what she likèd best.
And I believe some wench thou hast affected,
But woods and groves keep your faults undetected.
While thus I speak the waters more abounded,
And from the channel all abroad surrounded.
Mad stream, why dost our mutual joys defer?
Clown, from my journey why dost me deter?
How wouldst thou flow wert thou a noble flood,
If thy great fame in every region stood?
Thou hast no name, but com'st from snowy mountains;
No certain house thou hast, nor any fountains.
Thy springs are nought but rain and melted snow,
Which wealth cold winter doth on thee bestow.
Either th' art muddy in mid-winter tide,
Or full of dust dost on the dry earth slide.
What thirsty traveller ever drunk of thee?

Who said with grateful voice, 'Perpetual be'?
Harmful to beasts, and to the fields thou proves;
Perchance these others, me mine own loss moves.
To this I fondly loves of floods told plainly,
I shame so great names to have used so vainly.
I know not what expecting, I erewhile
Named Achelaus, Inachus, and Nile.
But for thy merits I wish thee, white stream,
Dry winters aye, and suns in heat extreme.

ELEGIA VI
Quod ab amica receptus cum ea coire non potuit, conqueritur

Either she was foul, or her attire was bad,
Or she was not the wench I wished t' have had.
Idly I lay with her, as if I loved not,
And like a burden grieved the bed that moved not.
Though both of us performed our true intent,
Yet could I not cast anchor where I meant.
She on my neck her ivory arms did throw,
Her arms far whiter than the Scythian snow,
And eagerly she kissed me with her tongue,
And under mine her wanton thigh she flung.
Yea, and she soothed me up, and called me 'Sir,'
And used all speech that might provoke and stir.
Yet like as if cold hemlock I had drunk,
It mockèd me, hung down the head, and sunk.
Like a dull cipher or rude block I lay,
Or shade or body was I, who can say?
What will my age do, age I cannot shun,
When in my prime my force is spent and done?
I blush, that being youthful, hot and lusty,
I prove neither youth nor man, but old and rusty.
Pure rose she, like a nun to sacrifice,
Or one that with her tender brother lies.
Yet boarded I the golden Chie twice,
And Libas, and the white cheeked Pitho thrice.
Corinna craved it in a summer's night,
And nine sweet bouts we had before daylight.
What, waste my limbs through some Thessalian charms?
May spells and drugs do silly souls such harms?
With virgin wax hath some imbased my joints,

And pierced my liver with sharp needles' points?
Charms change corn to grass and make it die;
By charms are running springs and fountains dry.
By charms mast drops from oaks, from vines grapes fall,
And fruit from trees when there's no wind at all.
Why might not then my sinews be enchanted,
And I grow faint as with some spirit haunted?
To this add shame: shame to perform it quailed me,
And was the second cause why vigour failed me.
My idle thoughts delighted her no more
Than did the robe or garment which she wore.
Yet might her touch make youthful Pylius fire,
And Tithon livelier than his years require.
Even her I had and she had me in vain,
What might I crave more, if I ask again?
I think the great gods grieved they had bestowed
The benefit which lewdly I forslowed.
I wished to be received in, in I get me;
To kiss, I kiss; to lie with her she let me.
Why was I blest? Why made king to refuse it?
Chuff-like had I not gold and could not use it?
So in a spring thirsts he that told so much,
And looks upon the fruits he cannot touch.
Hath any rose so from a fresh young maid,
As she might straight have gone to church and prayed?
Well, I believe she kissed not as she should,
Nor used the sleight and cunning which she could.
Huge oaks, hard adamants might she have moved,
And with sweet words cause deaf rocks to have loved.
Worthy she was to move both gods and men,
But neither was I man nor livèd then.
Can deaf ear take delight when Phaemius sings,
Or Thamyris in curious painted things?
What sweet thought is there but I had the same?
And one gave place still as another came.
Yet notwithstanding, like one dead it lay,
Drooping more than a rose pulled yesterday.
Now, when he should not jet, he bolts upright,
And craves his task, and seeks to be at fight.
Lie down with shame, and see thou stir no more,
Seeing thou wouldst deceive me as before.
Thou cozenest me: by thee surprised am I,
And bide sore loss with endless infamy.

Nay more, the wench did not disdain a whit
To take it in her hand and play with it.
But when she saw it would by no means stand,
But still drooped down, regarding not her hand,
'Why mock'st thou me,' she cried, 'or being ill,
Who bade thee lie down here against thy will?
Either th' art witched with blood of frogs new dead,
Or jaded cam'st thou from some other's bed.'
With that, her loose gown on, from me she cast her;
In skipping out her naked feet much graced her.
And lest her maid should know of this disgrace,
To cover it, spilt water on the place.

ELEGIA VII
Quod ab amica non recipiatur, dolet

What man will now take liberal arts in hand,
Or think soft verse in any stead to stand?
Wit was sometimes more precious than gold,
Now poverty great barbarism we hold.
When our books did my mistress fair content,
I might not go whither my papers went.
She praised me, yet the gate shut fast upon her,
I here and there go, witty with dishonour.
See a rich chuff, whose wounds great wealth inferred,
For bloodshed knighted, before me preferred!
Fool, canst thou him in thy white arms embrace?
Fool, canst thou lie in his enfolding space?
Knowest not this head a helm was wont to bear?
This side that serves thee, a sharp sword did wear.
His left hand, whereon on gold doth ill alight,
A target bore; blood-sprinkled was his right.
Canst touch that hand wherewith someone lie dead?
Ah whither is thy breast's soft nature fled?
Behold the signs of ancient fight, his scars,
Whate'er he hath his body gained in wars.
Perhaps he'll tell how oft he slew a man,
Confessing this, why dost thou touch him then?
I, the pure priest of Phoebus and the Muses,
At thy deaf doors in verse sing my abuses.
Not what we slothful knew, let wise men learn,

But follow trembling camps and battles stern,
And for a good verse draw the first dart forth:
Homer without this shall be nothing worth.
Jove, being admonished gold had sovereign power,
To win the maid came in a golden shower.
Till then, rough was her father, she severe,
The posts of brass, the walls of iron were;
But when in gifts the wise adulterer came,
She held her lap ope to receive the same.
Yet when old Saturn heaven's rule possessed,
All gain in darkness the deep earth suppressed.
Gold, silver, iron's heavy weight, and brass,
In hell were harboured; here was found no mass.
But better things it gave, corn without ploughs,
Apples, and honey in oaks' hollow boughs.
With strong ploughshares no man the earth did cleave,
The ditcher no marks on the ground did leave,
Nor hanging oars the troubled seas did sweep;
Men kept the shore, and sailed not into deep.
Against thyself, man's nature, thou wert cunning,
And to thine own loss was thy wit swift running.
Why gird'st thy cities with a towered wall?
Why let'st discordant hands to armour fall?
What dost with seas? With th' earth thou wert content;
Why seek'st not heaven, the third realm, to frequent?
Heaven thou affects; with Romulus, temples brave
Bacchus, Alcides, and now Caesar have.
Gold from the earth instead of fruits we pluck;
Soldiers by blood to be enriched have luck.
Courts shut the poor out; wealth gives estimation;
Thence grows the judge, and knight of reputation.
All they possess: they govern fields and laws,
They manage peace, and raw war's bloody jaws.
Only our loves let not such rich churls gain;
'Tis well if some wench for the poor remain.
Now, Sabine-like, though chaste she seems to live,
One her commands, who many things can give.
For me, she doth keeper and husband fear;
If I should give, both would the house forbear.
If of scorned lovers god be venger just,
O let him change goods so ill got to dust.

ELEGIA VIII
Tibulli mortem deflet

       If Thetis and the Morn their sons did wail,
And envious Fates great goddesses assail,
Sad Elegia, thy woeful hairs unbind:
Ah now a name too true thou hast, I find.
Tibullus, thy work's poet, and thy fame,
Burns his dead body in the funeral flame.
Lo Cupid brings his quiver spoilèd quite,
His broken bow, his firebrand without light.
How piteously with drooping wings he stands,
And knocks his bare breast with self-angry hands.
The locks spread on his neck receive his tears,
And shaking sobs his mouth for speeches bears.
So at Aeneas' burial, men report,
Fair-facèd Iulus, he went forth thy court.
And Venus grieves, Tibullus' life being spent,
As when the wild boar Adon's groin had rent:
The gods' care we are called, and men of piety,
And some there be that think we have a deity.
Outrageous death profanes all holy things,
And on all creatures obscure darkness brings.
To Thracian Orpheus what did parents good,
Or songs amazing wild beasts of the wood?
Where Linus by his father Phoebus laid
To sing with his unequalled harp is said.
See Homer from whose fountain ever filled
Pierian dew to poets is distilled:
Him the last day in black Averne hath drowned;
Verses alone are with continuance crowned.
The work of poets lasts Troy's labour's fame,
And that slow web night's falsehood did unframe.
So Nemesis, so Delia famous are:
The one his first love, th' other his new care.
What profit to us hath our pure life bred?
What to have lain alone in empty bed?
When bad fates take good men, I am forbod
By secret thoughts to think there is a god.
Live godly, thou shalt die; though honour heaven,
Yet shall thy life be forcibly bereaven.
Trust in good verse: Tibullus feels death's pains,
Scarce rests of all what a small urn contains.

Thee, sacred poet, could sad flames destroy?
Nor fearèd they thy body to annoy?
The holy gods' gilt temples they might fire,
That durst to so great wickedness aspire.
Eryx' bright empress turned her looks aside,
And some, that she refrained tears, have denied.
Yet better is 't, than if Corcyra's isle
Had thee unknown interred in ground most vile.
Thy dying eyes here did thy mother close,
Nor did thy ashes her last off'rings lose.
Part of her sorrow here thy sister bearing
Comes forth her unkembered locks asunder tearing.
Nemesis and thy first wench join their kisses
With thine, nor this last fire their presence misses.
Delia departing, 'Happier loved,' she saith,
'Was I: thou liv'dst, while thou esteem'dst my faith.'
Nemesis answers, 'What's my loss to thee?
His fainting hand in death engraspèd me.'
If aught remains of us but name and spirit,
Tibullus doth Elysium's joy inherit.
Your youthful brows with ivy girt to meet him,
With Calvus, learn'd Catullus come, and greet him,
And thou, if falsely charged to wrong thy friend,
Gallus, that car'st not blood and life to spend.
With these thy soul walks: souls if death release,
The godly, sweet Tibullus doth increase.
Thy bones I pray may in the urn safe rest,
And may th' earth's weight thy ashes naught molest.

ELEGIA IX
Ad Cererem, conquerens quod eius sacris cum amica concumbere non permittatur

Come were the times of Ceres' sacrifice:
In empty bed alone my mistress lies.
Golden-haired Ceres, crowned with ears of corn,
Why are our pleasures by thy means forborne?
Thee, goddess, bountiful all nations judge,
Nor less at man's prosperity any grudge.
Rude husbandmen baked not their corn before,
Nor on the earth was known the name of floor;
On mast of oaks, first oracles, men fed,

This was their meat, the soft grass was their bed.
First Ceres taught the seed in fields to swell,
And ripe-eared corn with sharp-edged scythes to fell;
She first constrained bulls' necks to bear the yoke,
And untilled ground with crooked ploughshares broke.
Who thinks her to be glad at lovers' smart,
And worshipped by their pain and lying apart?
Nor is she, though she loves the fertile fields,
A clown, nor no love from her warm breast yields.
Be witness Crete (nor Crete doth all things feign),
Crete proud that Jove her nursery maintain.
There he who rules the world's star-spangled towers,
A little boy, drunk teat-distilling showers.
Faith to the witness Jove's praise doth apply;
Ceres, I think, no known fault will deny.
The goddess saw Iasion on Candian Ide,
With strong hand striking wild beasts' bristled hide;
She saw, and as her marrow took the flame,
Was divers ways distract with love and shame.
Love conquered shame, the furrows dry were burned,
And corn with least part of itself returned.
When well-tossed mattocks did the ground prepare,
Being fit broken with the crooked share,
And seeds were equally in large fields cast,
The ploughman's hopes were frustrate at the last.
The grain-rich goddess in high woods did stray,
Her long hair's ear-wrought garland fell away.
Only was Crete fruitful that plenteous year;
Where Ceres went, each place was harvest there.
Ida, the seat of groves, did sing with corn,
Which by the wild boar in the woods was shorn.
Law-giving Minos did such years desire,
And wished the goddess long might feel love's fire.
Ceres, what sports to thee so grievous were,
As in thy sacrifice we them forbear?
Why am I sad, when Proserpine is found,
And Juno-like with Dis reigns underground?
Festival days ask Venus, songs and wine,
These gifts are meet to please the powers divine.

ELEGIA X
Ad amicam, a cuius amore discedere non potest

> Long have I borne much, mad thy faults me make:
> Dishonest love, my wearied breast forsake!
> Now have I freed myself, and fled the chain,
> And what I have borne, shame to bear again.
> We vanquish, and tread tamed Love under feet,
> Victorious wreaths at length my temples greet.
> Suffer, and harden: good grows by this grief,
> Oft bitter juice brings to the sick relief.
> I have sustained so oft thrust from the door,
> To lay my body on the hard moist floor.
> I know not whom thou lewdly didst embrace,
> When I to watch supplied a servant's place;
> I saw when forth a tired lover went,
> His side past service, and his courage spent.
> Yet this is less than if he had seen me;
> May that shame fall mine enemies' chance to be.
> When have not I, fixed to thy side, close laid?
> I have thy husband, guard, and fellow played.
> The people by my company she pleased;
> My love was cause that more men's love she seized.
> What should I tell her vain tongue's filthy lies,
> And, to my loss, god-wronging perjuries?
> What secret becks in banquets with her youths,
> With privy signs, and talk dissembling truths?
> Hearing her to be sick, I thither ran,
> But with my rival sick she was not then.
> These hardened me, with what I keep obscure;
> Some other seek, who will these things endure.
> Now my ship in the wishèd haven crowned,
> With joy hears Neptune's swelling waters sound.
> Leave thy once powerful words, and flatteries;
> I am not as I was before, unwise.
> Now love and hate my light breast each way move,
> But victory, I think, will hap to love.
> I'll hate, if I can; if not, love 'gainst my will:
> Bulls hate the yoke, yet what they hate have still.
> I fly her lust, but follow beauty's creature;
> I loathe her manners, love her body's feature.
> Nor with thee, nor without thee can I live,
> And doubt to which desire the palm to give.

Or less fair, or less lewd would thou mightst be;
Beauty with lewdness doth right ill agree.
Her deeds gain hate, her face entreateth love;
Ah, she doth more worth than her vices prove.
Spare me, O by our fellow-bed, by all
The gods who by thee to be perjured fall,
And by thy face to me a power divine,
And by thine eyes whose radiance burns out mine.
Whate'er thou art, mine art thou: choose this course,
Wilt have me willing, or to love by force?
Rather I'll hoist up sail, and use the wind,
That I may love yet, though against my mind.

ELEGIA XI

*Dolet amicam suam ita suis carminibus innotuisse ut rivales multos
sibi pararit*

What day was that which, all sad haps to bring,
White birds to lovers did not always sing?
Or is I think my wish against the stars?
Or shall I plain some god against me wars?
Who mine was called, whom I loved more than any,
I fear with me is common now to many.
Err I? Or by my books is she so known?
'Tis so: by my wit her abuse is grown.
And justly: for her praise why did I tell?
The wench by my fault is set forth to sell.
The bawd I play, lovers to her I guide:
Her gate by my hands is set open wide.
'Tis doubtful whether verse avail or harm,
Against my good they were an envious charm.
When Thebes, when Troy, when Caesar should be writ,
Alone Corinna moves my wanton wit.
With Muse opposed, would I my lines had done,
And Phoebus had forsook my work begun.
Nor, as use will not poets' record hear,
Would I my words would any credit bear.
Scylla by us her father's rich hair steals,
And Scylla's womb mad raging dogs conceals.
We cause feet fly, we mingle hairs with snakes,
Victorious Perseus a winged steed's back takes.
Our verse great Tityus a huge space outspreads,

And gives the viper-curlèd dog three heads.
We make Enceladus use a thousand arms,
And men enthralled by mermaids' singing charms.
The east winds in Ulysses' bags we shut,
And blabbing Tantalus in mid-waters put.
Niobe flint, Callist we make a bear,
Bird-changèd Progne doth her Itys tear;
Jove turns himself into a swan, or gold,
Or his bull's horns Europa's hand doth hold.
Proteus what should I name? Teeth, Thebes' first seed?
Oxen in whose mouths burning flames did breed?
Heav'n star Electra, that bewailed her sisters?
The ships whose godhead in the sea now glisters?
The sun turned back from Atreus' cursed table?
And sweet touched harp that to move stones was able?
Poets' large power is boundless and immense,
Nor have their words true history's pretence.
And my wench ought to have seemed falsely praised.
Now your credulity harm to me hath raised.

ELEGIA XII
De Iunonis festo

       When fruit-filled Tuscia should a wife give me,
We touched the walls, Camillus, won by thee.
The priests to Juno did prepare chaste feasts,
With famous pageants, and their home-bred beasts.
To know their rites well recompensed my stay,
Though thither leads a rough steep hilly way.
There stands an old wood with thick trees dark clouded:
Who sees it grants some deity there is shrouded.
An altar takes men's incense and oblation,
An altar made after the ancient fashion.
Here, when the pipe with solemn tunes doth sound,
The annual pomp goes on the covered ground.
White heifers by glad people forth are led,
Which with the grass of Tuscan fields are fed,
And calves from whose feared front no threat'ning flies,
And little pigs, base hogsties' sacrifice,
And rams with horns their hard heads wreathèd back;
Only the goddess-hated goat did lack,
By whom disclosed, she in the high woods took,

Is said to have attempted flight forsook.
Now is the goat brought through the boys with darts,
And given to him that the first wound imparts.
Where Juno comes, each youth and pretty maid
Show large ways, with their garments there displayed.
Jewels and gold their virgin tresses crown,
And stately robes to their gilt feet hang down.
As is the use, the nuns in white veils clad,
Upon their heads the holy mysteries had.
When the chief pomp comes, loud the people hollow,
And she her vestal virgin priests doth follow.
Such was the Greek pomp, Agamemnon dead,
Which fact, and country wealth Halesus fled,
And having wandered now through sea and land,
Built walls high towered with a prosperous hand.
He to th' Hetrurians Juno's feast commended;
Let me, and them by it be aye befriended.

ELEGIA XIII
Ad amicam, si peccatura est, ut occulte peccet

Seeing thou art fair, I bar not thy false playing,
But let not me, poor soul, know of thy straying.
Nor do I give thee counsel to live chaste,
But that thou wouldst dissemble, when 'tis past.
She hath not trod awry that doth deny it.
Such as confess have lost their good names by it.
What madness is 't to tell night's pranks by day,
And hidden secrets openly to bewray?
The strumpet with the stranger will not do
Before the room be clear, and door put to.
Will you make shipwrack of your honest name,
And let the world be witness of the same?
Be more advised, walk as a puritan,
And I shall think you chaste, do what you can.
Slip still, only deny it when 'tis done,
And before folk immodest speeches shun.
The bed is for lascivious toyings meet;
There use all tricks, and tread shame under feet.
When you are up and dressed, be sage and grave,
And in the bed hide all the faults you have.
Be not ashamed to strip you, being there,

And mingle thighs, yours ever mine to bear.
There in your rosy lips my tongue entomb,
Practise a thousand sports when there you come.
Forbear no wanton words you there would speak,
And with your pastime let the bedstead creak.
But with your robes put on an honest face,
And blush, and seem as you were full of grace.
Deceive all; let me err, and think I am right,
And like a wittol think thee void of sleight.
Why see I lines so oft received and given?
This bed and that by tumbling made uneven?
Like one start up, your hair tossed and displaced,
And with a wanton's tooth your neck new-raced?
Grant this, that what you do I may not see;
If you weigh not ill speeches, yet weigh me.
My soul fleets when I think what you have done,
And thorough every vein doth cold blood run.
Then thee whom I must love, I hate in vain,
And would be dead, but dead with thee remain.
I'll not sift much, but hold thee soon excused,
Say but thou wert injuriously accused.
Though while the deed be doing you be took,
And I see when you ope the two-leaved book,
Swear I was blind, deny, if you be wise,
And I will trust your words more than mine eyes.
From him that yields, the palm is quickly got,
Teach but your tongue to say, 'I did it not,'
And being justified by two words, think
The cause acquits you not, but I that wink.

ELEGIA XIV
Ad Venerem, quod elegis finem imponat

            Tender Love's mother, a new poet get;
This last end to my elegies is set,
Which I, Peligny's foster-child, have framed
(Nor am I by such wanton toys defamed),
Heir of an ancient house, if help that can,
Not only by war's rage made gentleman.
In Virgil Mantua joys, in Catull Verone,
Of me Peligny's nation boasts alone,
Whom liberty to honest arms compelled,

When careful Rome in doubt their prowess held.
And some guest, viewing wat'ry Sulmo's walls,
Where little ground to be enclosed befalls,
'How such a poet could you bring forth?' says;
'How small soe'er, I'll you for greatest praise.'
Both loves to whom my heart long time did yield,
Your golden ensigns pluck out of my field.
Horned Bacchus greater fury doth distil,
A greater ground with great horse is to till.
Weak elegies, delightful Muse, farewell;
A work that after my death here shall dwell.

The Passionate Shepherd
to His Love

Come live with me, and be my love,
And we will all the pleasures prove
That valleys, groves, hills and fields,
Woods, or steepy mountain yields.

And we will sit upon the rocks,
Seeing the shepherds feed their flocks
By shallow rivers, to whose falls
Melodious birds sing madrigals.

And I will make thee beds of roses,
And a thousand fragrant posies,
A cap of flowers, and a kirtle,
Embroidered all with leaves of myrtle.

A gown made of the finest wool
Which from our pretty lambs we pull,
Fair linèd slippers for the cold,
With buckles of the purest gold.

A belt of straw and ivy-buds,
With coral clasps and amber studs,
And if these pleasures may thee move,
Come live with me, and be my love.

The shepherd swains shall dance and sing
For thy delight each May morning.
If these delights thy mind may move,
Then live with me, and be my love.

Hero and Leander

On Hellespont, guilty of true love's blood,
In view and opposite two cities stood,
Sea-borderers, disjoined by Neptune's might:
The one Abydos, the other Sestos hight.
At Sestos Hero dwelt; Hero the fair,
Whom young Apollo courted for her hair,
And offered as a dower his burning throne,
Where she should sit for men to gaze upon.
The outside of her garments were of lawn,
The lining purple silk, with gilt stars drawn;
Her wide sleeves green, and bordered with a grove,
Where Venus in her naked glory strove
To please the careless and disdainful eyes
Of proud Adonis that before her lies.
Her kirtle blue, whereon was many a stain,
Made with the blood of wretched lovers slain.
Upon her head she ware a myrtle wreath,
From whence her veil reached to the ground beneath.
Her veil was artificial flowers and leaves,
Whose workmanship both man and beast deceives.
Many would praise the sweet smell as she passed,
When 'twas the odour which her breath forth cast;
And there for honey bees have sought in vain,
And beat from thence, have lighted there again.
About her neck hung chains of pebble-stone,
Which lightened by her neck, like diamonds shone.
She ware no gloves, for neither sun nor wind
Would burn or parch her hands, but to her mind,

Or warm or cool them, for they took delight
To play upon those hands, they were so white.
Buskins of shells all silvered uséd she,
And branched with blushing coral to the knee,
Where sparrows perched, of hollow pearl and gold,
Such as the world would wonder to behold:
Those with sweet water oft her handmaid fills,
Which as she went would chirrup through the bills.
Some say for her the fairest Cupid pined,
And looking in her face, was strooken blind.
But this is true, so like was one the other,
As he imagined Hero was his mother;
And oftentimes into her bosom flew,
About her naked neck his bare arms threw,
And laid his childish head upon her breast,
And with still panting rocked, there took his rest.
So lovely fair was Hero, Venus' nun,
As Nature wept, thinking she was undone,
Because she took more from her than she left,
And of such wondrous beauty her bereft:
Therefore, in sign her treasure suffered wrack,
Since Hero's time hath half the world been black.
Amorous Leander, beautiful and young
(Whose tragedy divine Musaeus sung)
Dwelt at Abydos; since him dwelt there none
For whom succeeding times make greater moan.
His dangling tresses that were never shorn,
Had they been cut, and unto Colchos borne,
Would have allured the vent'rous youth of Greece
To hazard more than for the Golden Fleece.
Fair Cynthia wished his arms might be her sphere;
Grief makes her pale because she moves not there.
His body was as straight as Circe's wand;
Jove might have sipped out nectar from his hand.
Even as delicious meat is to the taste,
So was his neck in touching, and surpassed
The white of Pelops' shoulder. I could tell ye
How smooth his breast was, and how white his belly,
And whose immortal fingers did imprint
That heavenly path with many a curious dint
That runs along his back, but my rude pen
Can hardly blazon forth the loves of men,
Much less of powerful gods: let it suffice

That my slack muse sings of Leander's eyes,
Those orient cheeks and lips, exceeding his
That leapt into the water for a kiss
Of his own shadow, and despising many,
Died ere he could enjoy the love of any.
Had wild Hippolytus Leander seen,
Enamoured of his beauty had he been;
His presence made the rudest peasant melt,
That in the vast uplandish country dwelt.
The barbarous Thracian soldier, moved with nought,
Was moved with him, and for his favour sought.
Some swore he was a maid in man's attire,
For in his looks were all that men desire,
A pleasant smiling cheek, a speaking eye,
A brow for love to banquet royally;
And such as knew he was a man would say,
'Leander, thou art made for amorous play:
Why art thou not in love, and loved of all?
Though thou be fair, yet be not thine own thrall.'
            The men of wealthy Sestos every year,
For his sake whom their goddess held so dear,
Rose-cheeked Adonis, kept a solemn feast.
Thither resorted many a wand'ring guest
To meet their loves; such as had none at all
Came lovers home from this great festival.
For every street like to a firmament
Glistered with breathing stars, who where they went
Frighted the melancholy earth, which deemed
Eternal heaven to burn, for so it seemed,
As if another Phaëton had got
The guidance of the sun's rich chariot.
But far above the loveliest Hero shined,
And stole away th' enchanted gazer's mind;
For like sea nymphs' inveigling harmony,
So was her beauty to the standers by.
Nor that night-wand'ring, pale and watery star
(When yawning dragons draw her thirling car
From Latmus' mount up to the gloomy sky,
Where crowned with blazing light and majesty,
She proudly sits) more overrules the flood
Than she the hearts of those that near her stood.
Even as, when gaudy nymphs pursue the chase,
Wretched Ixion's shaggy-footed race,

Incensed with savage heat, gallop amain
From steep pine-bearing mountains to the plain:
So ran the people forth to gaze upon her,
And all that viewed her were enamoured on her.
And as in fury of a dreadful fight,
Their fellows being slain or put to flight,
Poor soldiers stand with fear of death dead-strooken,
So at her presence all surprised and tooken
Await the sentence of her scornful eyes;
He whom she favours lives, the other dies.
There might you see one sigh, another rage,
And some (their violent passions to assuage)
Compile sharp satires, but alas too late,
For faithful love will never turn to hate.
And many seeing great princes were denied,
Pined as they went, and thinking on her died.
On this feast day, O cursèd day and hour,
Went Hero thorough Sestos, from her tower
To Venus' temple, where unhappily,
As after chanced, they did each other spy.
So fair a church as this had Venus none:
The walls were of discoloured jasper stone,
Wherein was Proteus carvèd, and o'erhead
A lively vine of green sea agate spread;
Where by one hand light-headed Bacchus hung,
And with the other wine from grapes outwrung.
Of crystal shining fair the pavement was;
The town of Sestos called it Venus' glass.
There might you see the gods in sundry shapes,
Committing heady riots, incest, rapes:
For know, that underneath this radiant floor
Was Danae's statue in a brazen tower,
Jove slyly stealing from his sister's bed,
To dally with Idalian Ganymede,
And for his love Europa bellowing loud,
Or tumbling with the rainbow in a cloud;
Blood-quaffing Mars, heaving the iron net
Which limping Vulcan and his Cyclops set;
Love kindling fire, to burn such towns as Troy;
Sylvanus weeping for the lovely boy
That now is turned into a cypress tree,
Under whose shade the wood gods love to be.
And in the midst a silver altar stood;

There Hero sacrificing turtles' blood,
Vailed to the ground, vailing her eyelids close,
And modestly they opened as she rose:
Thence flew Love's arrow with the golden head,
And thus Leander was enamourèd.
Stone still he stood, and evermore he gazed,
Till with the fire that from his count'nance blazed
Relenting Hero's gentle heart was strook:
Such force and virtue hath an amorous look.
      It lies not in our power to love or hate,
For will in us is overruled by fate.
When two are stripped, long ere the course begin
We wish that one should lose, the other win;
And one especially do we affect
Of two gold ingots like in each respect.
The reason no man knows: let it suffice,
What we behold is censured by our eyes.
Where both deliberate, the love is slight;
Who ever loved, that loved not at first sight?
      He kneeled, but unto her devoutly prayed;
Chaste Hero to herself thus softly said:
'Were I the saint he worships, I would hear him,'
And as she spake those words, came somewhat near him.
He started up, she blushed as one ashamed;
Wherewith Leander much more was inflamed.
He touched her hand, in touching it she trembled:
Love deeply grounded hardly is dissembled.
These lovers parlèd by the touch of hands;
True love is mute, and oft amazèd stands.
Thus while dumb signs their yielding hearts entangled,
The air with sparks of living fire was spangled,
And Night, deep-drenched in misty Acheron,
Heaved up her head, and half the world upon
Breathed darkness forth (dark night is Cupid's day).
And now begins Leander to display
Love's holy fire, with words, with sighs and tears,
Which like sweet music entered Hero's ears,
And yet at every word she turned aside,
And always cut him off as he replied.
At last, like to a bold sharp sophister,
With cheerful hope thus he accosted her.
      'Fair creature, let me speak without offence,
I would my rude words had the influence

To lead thy thoughts, as thy fair looks do mine,
Then shouldst thou be his prisoner, who is thine.
Be not unkind and fair; misshapen stuff
Are of behaviour boisterous and rough.
O shun me not, but hear me ere you go,
God knows I cannot force love, as you do.
My words shall be as spotless as my youth,
Full of simplicity and naked truth.
This sacrifice (whose sweet perfume descending
From Venus' altar to your footsteps bending)
Doth testify that you exceed her far,
To whom you offer, and whose nun you are.
Why should you worship her? Her you surpass
As much as sparkling diamonds flaring glass.
A diamond set in lead his worth retains;
A heavenly nymph, beloved of human swains,
Receives no blemish, but oft-times more grace,
Which makes me hope, although I am but base,
Base in respect of thee, divine and pure,
Dutiful service may thy love procure;
And I in duty will excel all other,
As thou in beauty dost exceed Love's mother.
Nor heaven, nor thou, were made to gaze upon;
As heaven preserves all things, so save thou one.
A stately builded ship, well-rigged and tall,
The ocean maketh more majestical:
Why vowest thou then to live in Sestos here,
Who on Love's seas more glorious wouldst appear?
Like untuned golden strings all women are,
Which long time lie untouched will harshly jar.
Vessels of brass oft handled brightly shine;
What difference betwixt the richest mine
And basest mould but use? For both, not used,
Are of like worth. Then treasure is abused
When misers keep it; being put to loan,
In time it will return us two for one.
Rich robes themselves and others do adorn;
Neither themselves nor others, if not worn.
Who builds a palace and rams up the gate,
Shall see it ruinous and desolate.
Ah simple Hero, learn thyself to cherish;
Lone women like to empty houses perish.
Less sins the poor rich man that starves himself

In heaping up a mass of drossy pelf,
Than such as you: his golden earth remains,
Which, after his decease, some other gains;
But this fair gem, sweet in the loss alone,
When you fleet hence, can be bequeathed to none.
Or if it could, down from th' enamelled sky
All heaven would come to claim this legacy,
And with intestine broils the world destroy,
And quite confound nature's sweet harmony.
Well therefore by the gods decreed it is,
We human creatures should enjoy that bliss.
One is no number; maids are nothing then,
Without the sweet society of men.
Wilt thou live single still? One shalt thou be,
Though never-singling Hymen couple thee.
Wild savages, that drink of running springs,
Think water far excels all earthly things:
But they that daily taste neat wine, despise it.
Virginity, albeit some highly prize it,
Compared with marriage, had you tried them both,
Differs as much as wine and water doth.
Base bullion for the stamp's sake we allow,
Even so for men's impression do we you.
By which alone, our reverend fathers say,
Women receive perfection every way.
This idol which you term virginity
Is neither essence subject to the eye,
No, nor to any one exterior sense,
Nor hath it any place of residence,
Nor is 't of earth or mould celestial,
Or capable of any form at all.
Of that which hath no being, do not boast;
Things that are not at all, are never lost.
Men foolishly do call it virtuous:
What virtue is it that is born with us?
Much less can honour be ascribed thereto,
Honour is purchased by the deeds we do.
Believe me, Hero, honour is not won,
Until some honourable deed be done.
Seek you for chastity, immortal fame,
And know that some have wronged Diana's name?
Whose name is it, if she be false or not,
So she be fair, but some vile tongues will blot?

But you are fair (aye me) so wondrous fair,
So young, so gentle, and so debonair,
As Greece will think, if thus you live alone,
Some one or other keeps you as his own.
Then, Hero, hate me not, nor from me fly,
To follow swiftly blasting infamy.
Perhaps thy sacred priesthood makes thee loth,
Tell me, to whom mad'st thou that heedless oath?'
     'To Venus,' answered she, and as she spake,
Forth from those two translucent cisterns brake
A stream of liquid pearl, which down her face
Made milk-white paths, whereon the gods might trace
To Jove's high court. He thus replied: 'The rites
In which Love's beauteous empress most delights,
Are banquets, Doric music, midnight revel,
Plays, masques, and all that stern age counteth evil.
Thee as a holy idiot doth she scorn,
For thou in vowing chastity hast sworn
To rob her name and honour, and thereby
Commit'st a sin far worse than perjury,
Even sacrilege against her deity,
Through regular and formal purity.
To expiate which sin, kiss and shake hands,
Such sacrifice as this Venus demands.'
     Thereat she smiled, and did deny him so,
As put thereby, yet might he hope for mo.
Which makes him quickly reinforce his speech,
And her in humble manner thus beseech:
     "Though neither gods nor men may thee deserve,
Yet for her sake whom you have vowed to serve,
Abandon fruitless cold virginity,
The gentle queen of Love's sole enemy.
Then shall you most resemble Venus' nun,
When Venus' sweet rites are performed and done.
Flint-breasted Pallas joys in single life,
But Pallas and your mistress are at strife.
Love, Hero, then, and be not tyrannous,
But heal the heart that thou hast wounded thus,
Nor stain thy youthful years with avarice;
Fair fools delight to be accounted nice.
The richest corn dies if it be not reaped;
Beauty alone is lost, too warily kept.'
These arguments he used, and many more,

Wherewith she yielded, that was won before.
Hero's looks yielded, but her words made war;
Women are won when they begin to jar.
Thus having swallowed Cupid's golden hook,
The more she strived, the deeper was she strook.
Yet evilly feigning anger, strove she still,
And would be thought to grant against her will.
So having paused a while, at last she said:
'Who taught thee rhetoric to deceive a maid?
Aye me, such words as these should I abhor,
And yet I like them for the orator.'
   With that Leander stooped, to have embraced her,
But from his spreading arms away she cast her,
And thus bespake him: 'Gentle youth, forbear
To touch the sacred garments which I wear.
   Upon a rock, and underneath a hill,
Far from the town (where all is whist and still,
Save that the sea, playing on yellow sand,
Sends forth a rattling murmur to the land,
Whose sound allures the golden Morpheus
In silence of the night to visit us)
My turret stands, and there God knows I play
With Venus' swans and sparrows all the day.
A dwarfish beldam bears me company,
That hops about the chamber where I lie,
And spends the night (that might be better spent)
In vain discourse and apish merriment.
Come thither.' As she spake this, her tongue tripped,
For unawares 'Come thither' from her slipped,
And suddenly her former colour changed,
And here and there her eyes through anger ranged.
And like a planet, moving several ways
At one self instant, she poor soul assays,
Loving, not to love at all, and every part
Strove to resist the motions of her heart.
And hands so pure, so innocent, nay such
As might have made heaven stoop to have a touch,
Did she uphold to Venus, and again
Vowed spotless chastity, but all in vain.
Cupid beats down her prayers with his wings,
Her vows above the empty air he flings;
All deep enraged, his sinewy bow he bent,
And shot a shaft that burning from him went,

Wherewith she strooken looked so dolefully,
As made Love sigh to see his tyranny.
And as she wept, her tears to pearl he turned,
And wound them on his arm, and for her mourned.
Then towards the palace of the Destinies
Laden with languishment and grief he flies,
And to those stern nymphs humbly made request
Both might enjoy each other, and be blest.
But with a ghastly dreadful countenance,
Threat'ning a thousand deaths at every glance,
They answered Love, nor would vouchsafe so much
As one poor word, their hate to him was such.
Hearken awhile, and I will tell you why.
Heaven's wingèd herald, Jove-borne Mercury,
The self-same day that he asleep had laid
Enchanted Argus, spied a country maid,
Whose careless hair, instead of pearl t' adorn it,
Glistered with dew, as one that seemed to scorn it.
Her breath as fragrant as the morning rose,
Her mind pure, and her tongue untaught to glose,
Yet proud she was (for lofty Pride that dwells
In towered courts is oft in shepherds' cells),
And too too well the fair vermilion knew,
And silver tincture of her cheeks, that drew
The love of every swain. On her this god
Enamoured was, and with his snaky rod
Did charm her nimble feet, and made her stay,
The while upon a hillock down he lay,
And sweetly on his pipe began to play,
And with smooth speech her fancy to assay,
Till in his twining arms he locked her fast,
And then he wooed with kisses, and at last,
As shepherds so, her on the ground he laid,
And tumbling in the grass, he often strayed
Beyond the bounds of shame, in being bold
To eye those parts which no eye should behold.
And like an insolent commanding lover,
Boasting his parentage, would needs discover
The way to new Elysium; but she,
Whose only dower was her chastity,
Having striv'n in vain, was now about to cry,
And crave the help of shepherds that were nigh.
Herewith he stayed his fury, and began

To give her leave to rise; away she ran,
After went Mercury, who used such cunning,
As she, to hear his tale, left off her running.
Maids are not won by brutish force and might,
But speeches full of pleasure and delight.
And, knowing Hermes courted her, was glad
That she such loveliness and beauty had
As could provoke his liking, yet was mute,
And neither would deny nor grant his suit.
Still vowed he love; she, wanting no excuse
To feed him with delays, as women use,
Or thirsting after immortality—
All women are ambitious naturally—
Imposed upon her lover such a task
As he ought not perform, nor yet she ask.
A draught of flowing nectar she requested,
Wherewith the king of gods and men is feasted.
He ready to accomplish what she willed,
Stole some from Hebe (Hebe Jove's cup filled)
And gave it to his simple rustic love;
Which being known (as what is hid from Jove?)
He inly stormed, and waxed more furious
Than for the fire filched by Prometheus,
And thrusts him down from heaven; he wand'ring here,
In mournful terms, with sad and heavy cheer,
Complained to Cupid. Cupid for his sake,
To be revenged on Jove did undertake,
And those on whom heaven, earth, and hell relies,
I mean the adamantine Destinies,
He wounds with love, and forced them equally
To dote upon deceitful Mercury.
They offered him the deadly fatal knife
That shears the slender threads of human life;
At his fair feathered feet the engines laid,
Which th' earth from ugly Chaos' den upweighed.
These he regarded not, but did entreat
That Jove, usurper of his father's seat,
Might presently be banished into hell,
And agèd Saturn in Olympus dwell.
They granted what he craved, and once again
Saturn and Ops began their golden reign.
Murder, rape, war, lust and treachery
Were with Jove closed in Stygian empery.

But long this blessèd time continued not:
As soon as he his wishèd purpose got,
He reckless of his promise did despise
The love of th' everlasting Destinies.
They seeing it, both Love and him abhorred,
And Jupiter unto his place restored.
And but that Learning, in despite of Fate,
Will mount aloft, and enter heaven gate,
And to the seat of Jove itself advance,
Hermes had slept in hell with Ignorance.
Yet as a punishment they added this,
That he and Poverty should always kiss.
And to this day is every scholar poor;
Gross gold from them runs headlong to the boor.
Likewise the angry Sisters, thus deluded,
To venge themselves on Hermes, have concluded
That Midas' brood shall sit in Honour's chair,
To which the Muses' sons are only heir:
And fruitful wits that inaspiring are
Shall discontent run into regions far.
And few great lords in virtuous deeds shall joy,
But be surprised with every garish toy,
And still enrich the lofty servile clown,
Who with encroaching guile keeps learning down.
Then muse not Cupid's suit no better sped,
Seeing in their loves the Fates were injurèd.
　　　　By this, sad Hero, with love unacquainted,
Viewing Leander's face, fell down and fainted.
He kissed her, and breathed life into her lips,
Wherewith, as one displeased, away she trips.
Yet as she went, full often looked behind,
And many poor excuses did she find
To linger by the way, and once she stayed,
And would have turned again, but was afraid,
In offering parley, to be counted light.
So on she goes, and in her idle flight,
Her painted fan of curlèd plumes let fall,
Thinking to train Leander therewithal.
He being a novice, knew not what she meant,
But stayed, and after her a letter sent,
Which joyful Hero answered in such sort,
As he had hope to scale the beauteous fort
Wherein the liberal Graces locked their wealth,

And therefore to her tower he got by stealth.
Wide open stood the door, he need not climb,
And she herself before the pointed time
Had spread the board, with roses strewed the room,
And oft looked out, and mused he did not come.
At last he came; O who can tell the greeting
These greedy lovers had at their first meeting?
He asked, she gave, and nothing was denied;
Both to each other quickly were affied.
Look how their hands, so were their hearts united,
And what he did she willingly requited.
(Sweet are the kisses, the embracements sweet,
When like desires and affections meet,
For from the earth to heaven is Cupid raised,
Where fancy is in equal balance peised.)
Yet she this rashness suddenly repented
And turned aside, and to herself lamented,
As if her name and honour had been wronged
By being possessed of him for whom she longed;
Ay, and she wished, albeit not from her heart,
That he would leave her turret and depart.
The mirthful god of amorous pleasure smiled
To see how he his captive nymph beguiled;
For hitherto he did but fan the fire,
And kept it down that it might mount the higher.
Now waxed she jealous, lest his love abated,
Fearing her own thoughts made her to be hated.
Therefore unto him hastily she goes,
And, like light Salmacis, her body throws
Upon his bosom, where with yielding eyes
She offers up herself a sacrifice,
To slake his anger, if he were displeased.
O what god would not therewith be appeased?
Like Aesop's cock, this jewel he enjoyèd,
And as a brother with his sister toyèd,
Supposing nothing else was to be done,
Now he her favour and good will had won.
But know you not that creatures wanting sense
By nature have a mutual appetence,
And wanting organs to advance a step,
Moved by Love's force, unto each other leap?
Much more in subjects having intellect
Some hidden influence breeds like effect.

Albeit Leander, rude in love, and raw,
Long dallying with Hero, nothing saw
That might delight him more, yet he suspected
Some amorous rites or other were neglected.
Therefore unto his body hers he clung;
She, fearing on the rushes to be flung,
Strived with redoubled strength; the more she strivèd,
The more a gentle pleasing heat revivèd,
Which taught him all that elder lovers know.
And now the same 'gan so to scorch and glow,
As in plain terms (yet cunningly) he craved it;
Love always makes those eloquent that have it.
She, with a kind of granting, put him by it,
And ever as he thought himself most nigh it,
Like to the tree of Tantalus she fled,
And, seeming lavish, saved her maidenhead.
Ne'er king more sought to keep his diadem,
Than Hero this inestimable gem.
Above our life we love a steadfast friend,
Yet when a token of great worth we send,
We often kiss it, often look thereon,
And stay the messenger that would be gone:
No marvel, then, though Hero would not yield
So soon to part from that she dearly held.
Jewels being lost are found again, this never;
'Tis lost but once, and once lost, lost for ever.
　　　　Now had the Morn espied her lover's steeds,
Whereat she starts, puts on her purple weeds,
And red for anger that he stayed so long,
All headlong throws herself the clouds among.
And now Leander, fearing to be missed,
Embraced her suddenly, took leave, and kissed.
Long was he taking leave, and loth to go,
And kissed again, as lovers use to do.
Sad Hero wrung him by the hand, and wept,
Saying, 'Let your vows and promises be kept.'
Then standing at the door, she turned about,
As loth to see Leander going out.
And now the sun, that through th' horizon peeps,
As pitying these lovers, downward creeps,
So that in silence of the cloudy night,
Though it was morning, did he take his flight.
But what the secret trusty night concealed,

Leander's amorous habit soon revealed:
With Cupid's myrtle was his bonnet crowned,
About his arms the purple riband wound
Wherewith she wreathed her largely spreading hair;
Nor could the youth abstain, but he must wear
The sacred ring wherewith she was endowed
When first religious chastity she vowed;
Which made his love through Sestos to be known,
And thence unto Abydos sooner blown
Than he could sail; for incorporeal Fame,
Whose weight consists in nothing but her name,
Is swifter than the wind, whose tardy plumes
Are reeking water, and dull earthly fumes.
Home when he came, he seemed not to be there,
But like exilèd air thrust from his sphere,
Set in a foreign place; and straight from thence,
Alcides-like, by mighty violence,
He would have chased away the swelling main,
That him from her unjustly did detain.
Like as the sun in a diameter
Fires and inflames objects removèd far
And heateth kindly, shining lat'rally,
So beauty sweetly quickens when 'tis nigh,
But being separated and removed,
Burns where it cherished, murders where it loved.
Therefore even as an index to a book,
So to his mind was young Leander's look.
O none but gods have power their love to hide,
Affection by the count'nance is descried.
The light of hidden fire itself discovers,
And love that is concealed betrays poor lovers.
His secret flame apparently was seen,
Leander's father knew where he had been,
And for the same mildly rebuked his son,
Thinking to quench the sparkles new begun.
But love resisted once, grows passionate,
And nothing more than counsel lovers hate.
For as a hot proud horse highly disdains
To have his head controlled, but breaks the reins,
Spits forth the ringled bit, and with his hooves
Checks the submissive ground: so he that loves,
The more he is restrained, the worse he fares.
What is it now, but mad Leander dares?

'O Hero, Hero!' Thus he cried full oft,
And then he got him to a rock aloft,
Where having spied her tower, long stared he on 't,
And prayed the narrow toiling Hellespont
To part in twain, that he might come and go,
But still the rising billows answered 'No.'
With that he stripped him to the ivory skin,
And crying, 'Love, I come,' leapt lively in.
Whereat the sapphire-visaged god grew proud,
And made his capering Triton sound aloud,
Imagining that Ganymede, displeased,
Had left the heavens; therefore on him he seized.
Leander strived, the waves about him wound,
And pulled him to the bottom, where the ground
Was strewed with pearl, and in low coral groves
Sweet singing mermaids sported with their loves
On heaps of heavy gold, and took great pleasure
To spurn in careless sort the shipwrack treasure.
For here the stately azure palace stood
Where kingly Neptune and his train abode.
The lusty god embraced him, called him 'love',
And swore he never should return to Jove.
But when he knew it was not Ganymede,
For under water he was almost dead,
He heaved him up, and looking on his face,
Beat down the bold waves with his triple mace,
Which mounted up, intending to have kissed him,
And fell in drops like tears because they missed him.
Leander being up, began to swim,
And, looking back, saw Neptune follow him;
Whereat aghast, the poor soul 'gan to cry,
'O let me visit Hero ere I die.'
The god put Helle's bracelet on his arm,
And swore the sea should never do him harm.
He clapped his plump cheeks, with his tresses played,
And smiling wantonly, his love bewrayed.
He watched his arms, and as they opened wide
At every stroke, betwixt them would he slide
And steal a kiss, and then run out and dance,
And as he turned, cast many a lustful glance,
And threw him gaudy toys to please his eye,
And dive into the water, and there pry
Upon his breast, his thighs, and every limb,

And up again, and close beside him swim,
And talk of love. Leander made reply,
'You are deceived, I am no woman, I.'
Thereat smiled Neptune, and then told a tale,
How that a shepherd, sitting in a vale,
Played with a boy so fair and kind,
As for his love both earth and heaven pined;
That of the cooling river durst not drink,
Lest water nymphs should pull him from the brink;
And when he sported in the fragrant lawns,
Goat-footed satyrs and up-staring fawns
Would steal him thence. Ere half this tale was done,
'Ay me,' Leander cried, 'th' enamoured sun,
That now should shine on Thetis' glassy bower,
Descends upon my radiant Hero's tower.
O that these tardy arms of mine were wings!'
And as he spake, upon the waves he springs.
Neptune was angry that he gave no ear,
And in his heart revenging malice bare:
He flung at him his mace, but as it went,
He called it in, for love made him repent.
The mace returning back, his own hand hit,
As meaning to be venged for darting it.
When this fresh bleeding wound Leander viewed,
His colour went and came, as if he rued
The grief which Neptune felt. In gentle breasts
Relenting thoughts, remorse and pity rests.
And who have hard hearts and obdurate minds,
But vicious, harebrained and illit'rate hinds?
The god, seeing him with pity to be movèd,
Thereon concluded that he was belovèd.
(Love is too full of faith, too credulous,
With folly and false hope deluding us.)
Wherefore Leander's fancy to surprise,
To the rich Ocean for gifts he flies.
'Tis wisdom to give much, a gift prevails,
When deep persuading oratory fails.
By this, Leander being near the land,
Cast down his weary feet, and felt the sand.
Breathless albeit he were, he rested not
Till to the solitary tower he got,
And knocked, and called, at which celestial noise
The longing heart of Hero much more joys

Than nymphs and shepherds when the timbrel rings,
Or crooked dolphin when the sailor sings.
She stayed not for her robes, but straight arose,
And drunk with gladness to the door she goes,
Where seeing a naked man, she screeched for fear;
Such sights as this to tender maids are rare;
And ran into the dark herself to hide.
Rich jewels in the dark are soonest spied:
Unto her was he led, or rather drawn,
By those white limbs, which sparkled through the lawn.
The nearer that he came, the more she fled,
And seeking refuge, slipped into her bed.
Whereon Leander sitting, thus began,
Through numbing cold, all feeble, faint and wan:
  'If not for love, yet, love, for pity sake,
Me in thy bed and maiden bosom take;
At least vouchsafe these arms some little room,
Who, hoping to embrace thee, cheerly swum.
This head was beat with many a churlish billow,
And therefore let it rest upon thy pillow.'
Herewith affrighted Hero shrunk away,
And in her lukewarm place Leander lay,
Whose lively heat, like fire from heaven fet,
Would animate gross clay, and higher set
The drooping thoughts of base declining souls
Than dreary Mars carousing nectar bowls.
His hands he cast upon her like a snare;
She, overcome with shame and sallow fear,
Like chaste Diana when Actaeon spied her,
Being suddenly betrayed, dived down to hide her.
And as her silver body downward went,
With both her hands she made the bed a tent,
And in her own mind thought herself secure,
O'ercast with dim and darksome coverture.
And now she lets him whisper in her ear,
Flatter, entreat, promise, protest and swear,
Yet ever as he greedily assayed
To touch those dainties, she the harpy played,
And every limb did as a soldier stout
Defend the fort, and keep the foeman out.
For though the rising ivory mount he scaled,
Which is with azure circling lines empaled,
Much like a globe (a globe may I term this,

By which love sails to regions full of bliss),
Yet there with Sisyphus he toiled in vain,
Till gentle parley did the truce obtain.
Wherein Leander on her quivering breast
Breathless spoke something, and sighed out the rest;
Which so prevailed, as he with small ado
Enclosed her in his arms and kissed her too.
And every kiss to her was as a charm,
And to Leander as a fresh alarm,
So that the truce was broke, and she alas
(Poor silly maiden) at his mercy was.
Love is not full of pity (as men say)
But deaf and cruel where he means to prey.
Even as a bird, which in our hands we wring,
Forth plungeth, and oft flutters with her wing,
She trembling strove; this strife of hers (like that
Which made the world) another world begat
Of unknown joy. Treason was in her thought,
And cunningly to yield herself she sought.
Seeming not won, yet won she was at length,
In such wars women use but half their strength.
Leander now, like Theban Hercules,
Entered the orchard of th' Hesperides,
Whose fruit none rightly can describe but he
That pulls or shakes it from the golden tree.
And now she wished this night were never done,
And sighed to think upon th' approaching sun,
For much it grieved her that the bright daylight
Should know the pleasure of this blessèd night,
And them like Mars and Erycine displayed,
Both in each other's arms chained as they laid.
Again she knew not how to frame her look,
Or speak to him who in a moment took
That which so long, so charily she kept,
And fain by stealth away she would have crept,
And to some corner secretly have gone,
Leaving Leander in the bed alone.
But as her naked feet were whipping out,
He on the sudden clinged her so about
That mermaid-like unto the floor she slid;
One half appeared, the other half was hid.
Thus near the bed she blushing stood upright,
And from her countenance behold ye might

A kind of twilight break, which through the hair,
As from an orient cloud, glimpse here and there.
And round about the chamber this false morn
Brought forth the day before the day was born.
So Hero's ruddy cheek Hero betrayed,
And her all naked to his sight displayed,
Whence his admiring eyes more pleasure took
Than Dis on heaps of gold fixing his look.
By this Apollo's golden harp began
To sound forth music to the Ocean,
Which watchful Hesperus no sooner heard,
But he the day's bright-bearing car prepared
And ran before, as harbinger of light,
And with his flaring beams mocked ugly Night,
Till she, o'ercome with anguish, shame and rage,
Danged down to hell her loathsome carriage.

Desunt nonnulla

Lucan's First Book

Wars worse than civil on Thessalian plains,
And outrage strangling law, and people strong
We sing, whose conquering swords their own breasts
    launched,
Armies allied, the kingdom's league uprooted,
Th' affrighted world's force bent on public spoil,
Trumpets and drums like deadly threat'ning other,
Eagles alike displayed, darts answering darts.
            Romans, what madness, what huge lust of war,
Hath made barbarians drunk with Latin blood?
Now Babylon (proud through our spoil) should stoop,
While slaughtered Crassus' ghost walks unrevenged,
Will ye wage war, for which you shall not triumph?
Aye me, O what a world of land and sea
Might they have won whom civil broils have slain!
As far as Titan springs, where night dims heaven,
Aye, to the torrid zone where mid-day burns,
And where stiff winter, whom no spring resolves,
Fetters the Euxine Sea with chains of ice;
Scythia and wild Armenia had been yoked,
And they of Nilus' mouth (if there live any).
Rome, if thou take delight in impious war,
First conquer all the earth, then turn thy force
Against thyself: as yet thou wants not foes.
That now the walls of houses half-reared totter,
That rampires fallen down, huge heaps of stone
Lie in our towns, that houses are abandoned,
And few live that behold their ancient seats,

Italy many years hath lien untilled
And choked with thorns, that greedy earth wants hinds,
Fierce Pyrrhus, neither thou nor Hannibal
Art cause; no foreign foe could so afflict us;
These plagues arise from wreak of civil power.
But if for Nero (then unborn) the Fates
Would find no other means (and gods not slightly
Purchase immortal thrones, nor Jove joyed heaven
Until the cruel Giants' war was done)
We plain not heavens, but gladly bear these evils
For Nero's sake: Pharsalia groan with slaughter,
And Carthage souls be glutted with our bloods;
At Munda let the dreadful battles join;
Add, Caesar, to these ills, Perusian famine,
The Mutin toils, the fleet at Leuca sunk,
And cruel field near burning Aetna fought.
Yet Rome is much bound to these civil arms,
Which made thee emperor, thee (seeing thou, being old,
Must shine a star) shall heaven (whom thou lovest)
Receive with shouts, where thou wilt reign as king,
Or mount the sun's flame-bearing chariot,
And with bright restless fire compass the earth,
Undaunted though her former guide be changed;
Nature and every power shall give thee place,
What god it please thee be, or where to sway.
But neither choose the north t' erect thy seat,
Nor yet the adverse reeking southern pole,
Whence thou shouldst view thy Rome with squinting beams.
If any one part of vast heaven thou swayest,
The burdened axis with thy force will bend;
The midst is best; that place is pure and bright.
There, Caesar, mayst thou shine and no cloud dim thee,
Then men from war shall bide in league and ease,
Peace through the world from Janus' fane shall fly,
And bolt the brazen gates with bars of iron.
Thou, Caesar, at this instant art my god:
Thee if I invocate, I shall not need
To crave Apollo's aid or Bacchus' help,
Thy power inspires the Muse that sings this war.
        The causes first I purpose to unfold
Of these garboils, whence springs a long discourse,
And what made madding people shake off peace.
The Fates are envious, high seats quickly perish,

Under great burdens falls are ever grievous;
Rome was so great it could not bear itself.
So when this world's compounded union breaks,
Time ends, and to old Chaos all things turn,
Confusèd stars shall meet, celestial fire
Fleet on the floods, the earth shoulder the sea,
Affording it no shore, and Phoebe's wain
Chase Phoebus, and enraged affect his place,
And strive to shine by day, and full of strife
Dissolve the engines of the broken world.
All great things crush themselves; such end the gods
Allot the height of honour, men so strong
By land and sea no foreign force could ruin.
O Rome, thyself art cause of all these evils,
Thyself thus shivered out to three men's shares:
Dire league of partners in a kingdom last not.
O faintly-joined friends, with ambition blind,
Why join you force to share the world betwixt you?
While th' earth the sea, and air the earth sustains,
While Titan strives against the world's swift course,
Or Cynthia, night's queen, waits upon the day,
Shall never faith be found in fellow kings.
Dominion cannot suffer partnership;
This need no foreign proof nor far-fet story:
Rome's infant walls were steeped in brothers' blood;
Nor then was land, or sea, to breed such hate,
A town with one poor church set them at odds.
          Caesar's and Pompey's jarring love soon ended,
'Twas peace against their wills; betwixt them both
Stepped Crassus in, even as the slender Isthmus,
Betwixt the Aegean and the Ionian sea
Keeps each from other, but being worn away,
They both burst out, and each encounter other:
So whenas Crassus' wretched death, who stayed them,
Had filled Assyrian Carra's walls with blood,
His loss made way for Roman outrages.
Parthians, y' afflict us more than ye suppose:
Being conquered, we are plagued with civil war.
Swords share our empire; Fortune, that made Rome
Govern the earth, the sea, the world itself,
Would not admit two lords; for Julia,
Snatchèd hence by cruel fates with ominous howls,
Bare down to hell her son, the pledge of peace,

And all bands of that death-presaging alliance.
Julia, had heaven given thee longer life,
Thou hadst restrained thy headstrong husband's rage,
Yea, and thy father too, and, swords thrown down,
Made all shake hands as once the Sabines did;
Thy death broke amity, and trained to war
These captains emulous of each other's glory.
Thou fear'dst, great Pompey, that late deeds would dim
Old triumphs, and that Caesar's conquering France
Would dash the wreath thou wear'st for pirates' wrack.
Thee war's use stirred, and thoughts that always scorned
A second place; Pompey could bide no equal,
Nor Caesar no superior: which of both
Had justest cause unlawful 'tis to judge.
Each side had great partakers: Caesar's cause
The gods abetted, Cato liked the other.
Both differed much: Pompey was strook in years,
And by long rest forgot to manage arms,
And being popular sought by liberal gifts
To gain the light unstable commons' love,
And joyed to hear his theatre's applause;
He lived secure, boasting his former deeds,
And thought his name sufficient to uphold him,
Like to a tall oak in a fruitful field,
Bearing old spoils and conquerors' monuments,
Who though his root be weak, and his own weight
Keep him within the ground, his arms all bare,
His body (not his boughs) send forth a shade;
Though every blast it nod, and seem to fall,
When all the woods about stand bolt upright,
Yet he alone is held in reverence.
Caesar's renown for war was less, he restless,
Shaming to strive but where he did subdue;
When ire or hope provoked, heady and bold,
At all times charging home, and making havoc;
Urging his fortune, trusting in the gods,
Destroying what withstood his proud desires,
And glad when blood and ruin made him way:
So thunder which the wind tears from the clouds,
With crack of riven air and hideous sound
Filling the world, leaps out and throws forth fire,
Affrights poor fearful men, and blasts their eyes
With overthwarting flames, and raging shoots

Alongst the air, and, nought resisting it,
Falls, and returns, and shivers where it lights.
Such humours stirred them up; but this war's seed
Was even the same that wracks all great dominions.
When Fortune made us lords of all, wealth flowed,
And then we grew licentious and rude;
The soldiers' prey and rapine brought in riot;
Men took delight in jewels, houses, plate,
And scorned old sparing diet, and ware robes
Too light for women; Poverty (who hatched
Rome's greatest wits) was loathed, and all the world
Ransacked for gold, which breeds the world decay;
And then large limits had their butting lands,
The ground which Curius and Camillus tilled
Was stretched unto the fields of hinds unknown.
Again, this people could not brook calm peace,
Them freedom without war might not suffice;
Quarrels were rife, greedy desire, still poor,
Did vile deeds; then 'twas worth the price of blood,
And deemed renown to spoil their native town;
Force mastered right, the strongest governed all.
Hence came it that th' edicts were overruled,
That laws were broke, tribunes with consuls strove,
Sale made of offices, and people's voices
Bought by themselves and sold, and every year
Frauds and corruption in the field of Mars;
Hence interest and devouring usury sprang,
Faith's breach, and hence came war, to most men welcome.
    Now Caesar overpassed the snowy Alps;
His mind was troubled, and he aimed at war,
And coming to the ford of Rubicon,
At night in dreadful vision fearful Rome
Mourning appeared, whose hoary hairs were torn,
And on her turret-bearing head dispersed,
And arms all naked, who with broken sighs,
And staring, thus bespoke: 'What mean'st thou, Caesar?
Whither goes my standard? Romans if ye be,
And bear true hearts, stay here!' This spectacle
Strook Caesar's heart with fear, his hair stood up,
And faintness numbed his steps there on the brink.
He thus cried out: 'Thou thunderer that guard'st
Rome's mighty walls built on Tarpeian rock,
Yet gods of Phrygia and Iulus' line

Quirinus' rites and Latian Jove advanced
On Alba hill, O vestal flames, O Rome,
My thought's sole goddess, aid mine enterprise!
I hate thee not, to thee my conquests stoop;
Caesar is thine, so please it thee, thy soldier;
He, he afflicts Rome that made me Rome's foe.'
This said, he laying aside all lets of war,
Approached the swelling stream with drum and ensign;
Like to a lion of scorched desert Afric,
Who, seeing hunters, pauseth till fell wrath
And kingly rage increase, then having whisked
His tail athwart his back, and crest heaved up,
With jaws wide open ghastly roaring out
(Albeit the Moor's light javelin or his spear
Sticks in his side), yet runs upon the hunter.
      In summer time the purple Rubicon,
Which issues from a small spring, is but shallow,
And creeps along the values dividing just
The bounds of Italy from Cisalpine France;
But now the winter's wrath, and wat'ry moon
Being three days old, enforced the flood to swell,
And frozen Alps thawed with resolving winds.
The thunder-hoofed horse, in a crooked line,
To scape the violence of the stream, first waded,
Which being broke the foot had easy passage.
As soon as Caesar got unto the bank
And bounds of Italy, 'Here, here,' saith he,
'An end of peace; here end polluted laws;
Hence, leagues and covenants; Fortune, thee I follow,
War and the Destinies shall try my cause.'
This said, the restless general through the dark
(Swifter than bullets thrown from Spanish slings,
Or darts which Parthians backward shoot) marched on,
And then (when Lucifer did shine alone,
And some dim stars) he Ariminum entered.
Day rose, and viewed these tumults of the war;
Whether the gods or blust'ring south were cause
I know not, but the cloudy air did frown.
The soldiers having won the market-place,
There spread the colours, with confusèd noise
Of trumpet's clange, shrill cornets, whistling fifes.
The people started; young men left their beds,
And snatched arms near their household-gods hung up,

Such as peace yields: worm-eaten leathern targets
Through which the wood peered, headless darts, old swords
With ugly teeth of black rust foully scarred.
But seeing white eagles, and Rome's flags well known,
And lofty Caesar in the thickest throng,
They shook for fear, and cold benumbed their limbs,
And muttering much, thus to themselves complained:
'O walls unfortunate, too near to France,
Predestinate to ruin! All lands else
Have stable peace, here war's rage first begins,
We bide the first brunt. Safer might we dwell
Under the frosty Bear, or parching East,
Wagons or tents, than in this frontier town.
We first sustained the uproars of the Gauls
And furious Cimbrians, and of Carthage Moors;
As oft as Rome was sacked, here 'gan the spoil.'
Thus sighing whispered they, and none durst speak
And show their fear or grief; but as the fields,
When birds are silent thorough winter's rage,
Or sea far from the land, so all were whist.
Now light had quite dissolved the misty night,
And Caesar's mind unsettled musing stood;
But gods and Fortune pricked him to this war,
Infringing all excuse of modest shame,
And labouring to approve his quarrel good.
The angry Senate, urging Gracchus' deeds,
From doubtful Rome wrongly expelled the tribunes
That crossed them; both which now approached the camp,
And with them Curio, sometime tribune too,
One that was fee'd for Caesar, and whose tongue
Could tune the people to the nobles' mind.
'Caesar,' said he, 'while eloquence prevailed,
And I might plead, and draw the commons' minds
To favour thee, against the Senate's will,
Five years I lengthened thy command in France;
But law being put to silence by the wars,
We, from our houses driven, most willingly
Suffered exile: let thy sword bring us home.
Now, while their part is weak and fears, march hence:
Where men are ready, lingering ever hurts.
In ten years won'st thou France; Rome may be won
With far less toil, and yet the honour's more;
Few battles fought with prosperous success

May bring her down, and with her all the world.
Nor shalt thou triumph when thou com'st to Rome,
Nor Capitol be adorned with sacred bays.
Envy denies all; with thy blood must thou
Aby thy conquest past: the son decrees
To expel the father; share the world thou canst not;
Enjoy it all thou mayst.' Thus Curio spake,
And therewith Caesar, prone enough to war,
Was so incensed as are Eleius steeds
With clamours, who, though locked and chained in stalls,
Souse down the walls, and make a passage forth.
Straight summoned he his several companies
Unto the standard; his grave look appeased
The wrestling tumult, and right hand made silence,
And thus he spake: 'You that with me have borne
A thousand brunts, and tried me full ten years,
See how they quit our blood shed in the north,
Our friends' death, and our wounds, our wintering
Under the Alps! Rome rageth now in arms
As if the Carthage Hannibal were near.
Cornets of horse are mustered for the field,
Woods turned to ships; both land and sea against us.
Had foreign wars ill-thrived, or wrathful France
Pursued us hither, how were we bested,
When, coming conqueror, Rome afflicts me thus?
Let come their leaders whom long peace hath quailed,
Raw soldiers lately pressed, and troops of gowns;
Brabbling Marcellus; Cato whom fools reverence;
Must Pompey's followers, with strangers' aid
(Whom from his youth he bribed), needs make him king?
And shall he triumph long before his time,
And having once got head still shall he reign?
What should I talk of men's corn reaped by force,
And by him kept of purpose for a dearth?
Who sees not war sit by the quivering judge,
And sentence given in rings of naked swords,
And laws assailed, and armed men in the Senate?
'Twas his troop hemmed in Milo being accused;
And now, lest age might wane his state, he casts
For civil war, wherein through use he's known
To exceed his master, that arch-traitor Sulla.
A brood of barbarous tigers, having lapped
The blood of many a herd, whilst with their dams

They kenneled in Hircania, evermore
Will rage and prey: so Pompey, thou having licked
Warm gore from Sulla's sword, art yet athirst;
Jaws fleshed with blood continue murderous.
Speak, when shall this thy long-usurped power end?
What end of mischief? Sulla teaching thee,
At last learn, wretch, to leave thy monarchy.
What, now Sicilian pirates are suppressed,
And jaded king of Pontus poisoned slain,
Must Pompey as his last foe plume on me,
Because at his command I wound not up
My conquering eagles? Say I merit nought,
Yet, for long service done, reward these men,
And so they triumph, be 't with whom ye will.
Whither now shall these old bloodless souls repair?
What seats for their deserts? What store of ground
For servitors to till? What colonies
To rest their bones? Say, Pompey, are these worse
Than pirates of Sicilia? They had houses.
Spread, spread these flags that ten years' space have
    conquered!
Let's use our tried force; they that now thwart right,
In wars will yield to wrong: the gods are with us.
Neither spoil nor kingdom seek we by these arms,
But Rome at thraldom's feet to rid from tyrants.'
This spoke, none answered; but a murmuring buzz
Th' unstable people made: their household gods
And love to Rome (though slaughter steeled their hearts,
And minds were prone) restrained them; but war's love
And Caesar's awe dashed all. Then Laelius,
The chief centurion, crowned with oaken leaves
For saving of a Roman citizen,
Stepped forth, and cried: 'Chief leader of Rome's force,
So be I may be bold to speak a truth,
We grieve at this thy patience and delay.
What doubt'st thou us? Even now when youthful blood
Pricks forth our lively bodies, and strong arms
Can mainly throw the dart, wilt thou endure
These purple grooms, that Senate's tyranny?
Is conquest got by civil war so heinous?
Well, lead us then to Syrtes' desert shore,
Or Scythia, or hot Libya's thirsty sands.
This band, that all behind us might be quailed,

Hath with thee passed the swelling ocean,
And swept the foaming breast of Arctic's Rhene.
Love overrules my will, I must obey thee,
Caesar; he whom I hear thy trumpets charge
I hold no Roman; by these ten blest ensigns
And all thy several triumphs, shouldst thou bid me
Entomb my sword within my brother's bowels,
Or father's throat, or woman's groaning womb,
This hand (albeit unwilling) should perform it;
Or rob the gods, or sacred temples fire.
These troops should soon pull down the church of Jove.
If to encamp on Tuscan Tiber's streams,
I'll boldly quarter out the fields of Rome;
What walls thou wilt be levelled with the ground,
These hands shall thrust the ram, and make them fly,
Albeit the city thou wouldst have so razed
Be Rome itself.' Here every band applauded,
And with their hands held up all jointly cried
They'll follow where he please. The shouts rent heaven,
As when against pine-bearing Ossa's rocks
Beats Thracian Boreas, or when trees bow down
And rustling swing up as the wind fets breath.
       When Caesar saw his army prone to war,
And Fates so bent, lest sloth and long delay
Might cross him, he withdrew his troops from France,
And in all quarters musters men for Rome.
They by Lemannus' nook forsook their tents;
They whom the Lingones foiled with painted spears,
Under the rocks by crooked Vogesus;
And many came from shallow Isara,
Who, running long, falls in a greater flood,
And ere he sees the sea loseth his name;
The yellow Ruthens left their garrisons;
Mild Atax glad it bears not Roman boats,
And frontier Varus that the camp is far,
Sent aid; so did Alcides' port, whose seas
Eat hollow rocks, and where the north-west wind
Nor Zephyr rules not, but the north alone
Turmoils the coast, and enterance forbids;
And others came from that uncertain shore
Which is nor sea, nor land, but ofttimes both,
And changeth as the ocean ebbs and flows;
Whether the sea rolled always from that point

Whence the wind blows, still forcèd to and fro,
Or that the wandering main follow the moon,
Or flaming Titan (feeding on the deep)
Pulls them aloft, and makes the surge kiss heaven,
Philosophers, look you, for unto me,
Thou cause, whate'er thou be whom God assigns
This great effect, art hid. They came that dwell
By Nemes' fields, and banks of Satirus,
Where Tarbel's winding shores embrace the sea;
The Santons that rejoice in Caesar's love,
Those of Bituriges and light Axon pikes;
And they of Rhene and Leuca, cunning darters,
And Sequana that well could manage steeds;
The Belgians apt to govern British cars;
Th' Averni too, which boldly feign themselves
The Romans' brethren, sprung of Ilian race;
The stubborn Nervians stained with Cotta's blood,
And Vangions who, like those of Sarmata,
Wear open slops; and fierce Batavians,
Whom trumpets' clange incites, and those that dwell
By Cinga's stream, and where swift Rhodanus
Drives Araris to sea; they near the hills
Under whose hoary rocks Gebenna hangs;
And Trevier, thou being glad that wars are past thee;
And you, late-shorn Ligurians, who were wont
In large-spread hair to exceed the rest of France;
And where to Hesus and fell Mercury
They offer human flesh, and where Jove seems
Bloody like Dian, whom the Scythians serve.
And you, French Bardi, whose immortal pens
Renown the valiant souls slain in your wars,
Sit safe at home and chant sweet poesy.
And, Druides, you now in peace renew
Your barbarous customs and sinister rites;
In unfelled woods and sacred groves you dwell,
And only gods and heavenly powers you know,
Or only know you nothing. For you hold
That souls pass not to silent Erebus
Or Pluto's bloodless kingdom, but elsewhere
Resume a body: so (if truth you sing)
Death brings long life. Doubtless these northern men,
Whom death, the greatest of all fears, affright not,
Are blest by such sweet error; this makes them

Run on the sword's point and desire to die,
And shame to spare life which being lost is won.
You likewise that repulsed the Cayc foe,
March towards Rome; and you, fierce men of Rhene,
Leaving your country open to the spoil.
These being come, their huge power made him bold
To manage greater deeds; the bordering towns
He garrisoned, and Italy he filled with soldiers.
Vain fame increased true fear, and did invade
The people's minds, and laid before their eyes
Slaughter to come, and swiftly bringing news
Of present war, made many lies and tales.
One swears his troops of daring horsemen fought
Upon Mevania's plain, where bulls are grazed;
Other that Caesar's barbarous bands were spread
Along Nar flood that into Tiber falls,
And that his own ten ensigns and the rest
Marched not entirely, and yet hide the ground;
And that he's much changed, looking wild and big,
And far more barbarous than the French (his vassals)
And that he lags behind with them of purpose
Born 'twixt the Alps and Rhene, which he hath brought
From out their northern parts, and that Rome,
He looking on, by these men should be sacked.
Thus in his fright did each man strengthen Fame,
And, without ground, feared what themselves had feigned.
Nor were the commons only strook to heart
With this vain terror, but the Court, the Senate:
The fathers' selves leaped from their seats, and, flying,
Left hateful war decreed to both the consuls.
Then, with their fear and danger all distract,
Their sway of flight carries the heady rout
That in chained troops break forth at every port;
You would have thought their houses had been fired,
Or, dropping-ripe, ready to fall with ruin;
So rushed the inconsiderate multitude
Thorough the city, hurried headlong on,
As if the only hope that did remain
To their afflictions were t' abandon Rome.
Look how when stormy Auster from the breach
Of Libyan Syrtes rolls a monstrous wave,
Which makes the mainsail fall with hideous sound,
The pilot from the helm leaps in the sea,

And mariners, albeit the keel be sound,
Shipwrack themselves: even so, the city left,
All rise in arms, nor could the bedrid parents
Keep back their sons, or women's tears their husbands;
They stayed not either to pray or sacrifice,
Their household gods restrain them not, none lingered
As loth to leave Rome whom they held so dear;
Th' irrevocable people fly in troops.
O gods, that easy grant men great estates,
But hardly grace to keep them: Rome, that flows
With citizens and captives, and would hold
The world (were it together) is by cowards
Left as a prey, now Caesar doth approach.
When Romans are besieged by foreign foes,
With slender trench they escape night stratagems,
And sudden rampire raised of turf snatched up
Would make them sleep securely in their tents.
Thou, Rome, at name of war runn'st from thyself,
And wilt not trust thy city walls one night:
Well might these fear, when Pompey feared and fled.
Now evermore, lest some one hope might ease
The commons' jangling minds, apparent signs arose,
Strange sights appeared, the angry threat'ning gods
Filled both the earth and seas with prodigies;
Great store of strange and unknown stars were seen
Wandering about the north, and rings of fire
Fly in the air, and dreadful bearded stars,
And comets that presage the fall of kingdoms;
The flattering sky glittered in often flames,
And sundry fiery meteors blazed in heaven,
Now spear-like, long, now like a spreading torch;
Lightning in silence stole forth without clouds,
And from the northern climate snatching fire
Blasted the Capitol; the lesser stars,
Which wont to run their course through empty night,
At noonday mustered; Phoebe, having filled
Her meeting horns to match her brother's light,
Strook with th' earth's sudden shadow, waxèd pale;
Titan himself throned in the midst of heaven
His burning chariot plunged in sable clouds,
And whelmed the world in darkness, making men
Despair of day, as did Thyestes' town,
Mycenae, Phoebus flying through the east.

Fierce Mulciber unbarrèd Aetna's gate,
Which flamèd not on high, but headlong pitched
Her burning head on bending Hespery.
Coal-black Charybdis whirled a sea of blood;
Fierce mastiffs howled; the vestal fires went out;
The flame in Alba, consecrate to Jove,
Parted in twain, and with a double point
Rose like the Theban brothers' funeral fire;
The earth went off her hinges, and the Alps
Shook the old snow from off their trembling laps.
The ocean swelled as high as Spanish Calpe,
Or Atlas' head. Their saints and household gods
Sweat tears to show the travails of their city.
Crowns fell from holy statues, ominous birds
Defiled the day, and wild beasts were seen,
Leaving the woods, lodge in the streets of Rome.
Cattle were seen that muttered human speech;
Prodigous births with more and ugly joints
Than nature gives, whose sight appals the mother;
And dismal prophecies were spread abroad;
And they whom fierce Bellona's fury moves
To wound their arms, sing vengeance; Sibyl's priests,
Curling their bloody locks, howl dreadful things;
Souls quiet and appeased sighed from their graves;
Clashing of arms was heard; in untrod woods
Shrill voices shright, and ghosts encounter men.
Those that inhabited the suburb fields
Fled; foul Erinnys stalked about the walls,
Shaking her snaky hair and crooked pine
With flaming top, much like that hellish fiend
Which made the stern Lycurgus wound his thigh,
Or fierce Agave mad; or like Megaera
That scared Alcides, when by Juno's task
He had before looked Pluto in the face.
Trumpets were heard to sound; and with what noise
An armèd battle joins, such and more strange
Black night brought forth in secret: Sulla's ghost
Was seen to walk, singing sad oracles;
And Marius' head above cold Tav'ron peering
(His grave broke open) did affright the boors.
To these ostents (as their old custom was)
They call th' Etrurian augurs, amongst whom
The gravest, Arruns, dwelt in forsaken Luca,

Well skilled in pyromancy, one that knew
The hearts of beasts, and flight of wand'ring fowls.
First he commands such monsters Nature hatched
Against her kind (the barren mule's loathed issue)
To be cut forth and cast in dismal fires;
Then, that the trembling citizens should walk
About the city; then the sacred priests
That with divine lustration purged the walls,
And went the round, in and without the town.
Next, an inferior troop, in tucked-up vestures,
After the Gabine manner; then the nuns
And their veiled matron, who alone might view
Minerva's statue; then, they that keep and read
Sibylla's secret works, and washed their saint
In Almo's flood; next, learned augurs follow,
Apollo's soothsayers, and Jove's feasting priests,
The skipping Salii with shields like wedges,
And flamens last, with network woollen veils.
While these thus in and out had circled Rome,
Look, what the lightning blasted Arruns takes,
And it inters with murmurs dolorous,
And calls the place Bidental; on the altar
He lays a ne'er-yoked bull, and pours down wine,
Then crams salt leaven on his crooked knife;
The beast long struggled, as being like to prove
An awkward sacrifice, but by the horns
The quick priest pulled him on his knees and slew him.
No vein sprung out, but from the yawning gash,
Instead of red blood, wallowed venomous gore.
These direful signs made Arruns stand amazed,
And searching farther for the gods' displeasure,
The very colour scared him; a dead blackness
Ran through the blood, that turned it all to jelly,
And stained the bowels with dark loathsome spots;
The liver swelled with filth, and every vein
Did threaten horror from the host of Caesar;
A small thin skin contained the vital parts;
The heart stirred not, and from the gaping liver
Squeezed matter; through the caul the entrails peered,
And which (aye me) ever pretendeth ill,
At that bunch where the liver is, appeared
A knob of flesh, whereof one half did look
Dead and discoloured, th' other lean and thin.

By these he seeing what mischiefs must ensue
Cried out, 'O gods! I tremble to unfold
What you intend: great Jove is now displeased,
And in the breast of this slain bull are crept
Th' infernal powers. My fear transcends my words,
Yet more will happen than I can unfold.
Turn all to good, be augury vain, and Tages,
Th' art's master, false!' Thus, in ambiguous terms
Involving all, did Arruns darkly sing.
But Figulus, more seen in heavenly mysteries,
Whose like Egyptian Memphis never had
For skill in stars and tuneful planeting,
In this sort spake: 'The world's swift course is lawless
And casual; all the stars at random rage;
Or if Fate rule them, Rome, thy citizens
Are near some plague. What mischief shall ensue?
Shall towns be swallowed? Shall the thickened air
Become intemperate? Shall the earth be barren?
Shall water be congealed and turned to ice?
O gods, what death prepare ye? With what plague
Mean ye to rage? The death of many men
Meets in one period. If cold noisome Saturn
Were now exalted, and with blue beams shined,
Then Ganymede would renew Deucalion's flood,
And in the fleeting sea the earth be drenched.
O Phoebus, shouldst thou with thy rays now singe
The fell Nemean beast, th' earth would be fired,
And heaven tormented with thy chafing heat;
But thy fires hurt not. Mars, 'tis thou inflam'st
The threatening Scorpion with the burning tail,
And fir'st his cleyes. Why art thou thus enraged?
Kind Jupiter hath low declined himself;
Venus is faint; swift Hermes retrograde;
Mars only rules the heaven. Why do the planets
Alter their course, and vainly dim their virtue?
Sword-girt Orion's side glisters too bright:
War's rage draws near, and to the sword's strong hand
Let all laws yield, sin bear the name of virtue.
Many a year these furious broils let last;
Why should we wish the gods should ever end them?
War only gives us peace. O Rome, continue
The course of mischief, and stretch out the date
Of slaughter; only civil broils make peace.'

These sad presages were enough to scare
The quivering Romans, but worse things affright them.
As Maenas full of wine on Pindus raves,
So runs a matron through th' amazèd streets,
Disclosing Phoebus' fury in this sort:
'Paean, whither am I haled? Where shall I fall,
Thus borne aloft? I see Pangaeus' hill
With hoary top, and under Haemus' mount
Philippi plains. Phoebus, what rage is this?
Why grapples Rome, and makes war, having no foes?
Whither turn I now? Thou lead'st me toward th' east,
Where Nile augmenteth the Pelusian sea;
This headless trunk that lies on Nilus' sand
I know. Now throughout the air I fly
To doubtful Syrtes and dry Afric, where
A fury leads the Emathian bands; from thence
To the pine-bearing hills, hence to the mounts
Pyrene, and so back to Rome again.
See, impious war defiles the Senate-house,
New factions rise; now through the world again
I go; O Phoebus, how me Neptune's shore,
And other regions, I have seen Philippi.'
This said, being tired with fury she sunk down.